Southern Literary Studies
LOUIS D. RUBIN, JR., EDITOR

Walker Percy and the
Old Modern Age

Walker Percy and the Old Modern Age

REFLECTIONS ON
LANGUAGE,
ARGUMENT, AND THE
TELLING OF STORIES

Patricia Lewis Poteat

Louisiana State University Press
Baton Rouge and London

Copyright © 1985 by Louisiana State University Press
ALL RIGHTS RESERVED
Manufactured in the United States of America
Designer: Barbara Werden
Typeface: Linotron Sabon
Typesetter: G & S Typesetters, Inc.
Printer and binder: Edwards Brothers, Inc.

Publication of the book has been assisted by a grant from the Andrew W. Mellon Foundation.

Grateful acknowledgment is made to Farrar, Straus & Giroux, Inc. for permission to quote from *The Message in the Bottle*, © 1954, 1956, 1957, 1958, 1959, 1961, 1972, 1975 by Walker Percy; *The Last Gentleman*, © 1966 by Walker Percy; *Love in the Ruins*, © 1971 by Walker Percy; *Lancelot*, © 1977 by Walker Percy; *The Second Coming*, © 1980 by Walker Percy; and to Alfred A. Knopf, Inc., for permission to quote from *The Moviegoer*, © 1960 by Walker Percy. For reprint rights covering the British Commonwealth excluding Canada, acknowledgment is made to Martin Secker & Warburg Limited for the novels: *The Moviegoer*, *The Last Gentleman*, *Love in the Ruins*, *The Second Coming*, and *Lancelot*.

LIBRARY OF CONGRESS CATALOGING IN PUBLICATION DATA

Poteat, Patricia Lewis.
   Walker Percy and the old modern age.

   (Southern literary studies)
   Includes index.
   1. Percy, Walker, 1916–   —Criticism and
interpretation. 2. Percy, Walker, 1916–   —Philosophy.
3. Philosophy in literature. I. Title. II. Series.
PS3566.E6912Z83   1984   813'.54   84-10005
ISBN 0-8071-1187-2

FOR CHINA BOY

CONTENTS

ACKNOWLEDGMENTS

IN AN IMPORTANT and obvious sense, writing is a solitary enterprise. In an equally important but less obvious sense, however, it is a profoundly convivial one, its happy fruition possible only because colleagues, friends, and family give of their time, expertise, support, well-placed skepticism, and, perhaps most important, their patience. This work is no exception.

The list of persons to whom I owe special thanks must begin with two friends and colleagues who were and remain my most excellent teachers, James Ellis and Benjamin Ladner. From them I learned how to read and think about stories. In this way, if I may paraphrase Emerson, they gave me leave to be what I inly am. My debt to them is great.

Another special thanks must go to Thomas Langford and William Barrett, who read my manuscript in its early stages. For their astute comments, quiet encouragement, and, most important, for their stout faith that I was, as Binx Bolling might put it, "onto something," I thank them.

To my friends Sarah Barnhill, Farnum Brown, Wanda Camp, Martha Crunkleton, and Susan Schreiner—each of whom has helped me in ways which I cannot begin to name—thanks.

For resisting the temptation to despair of their exceedingly willful and most exhaustively educated child, the best thanks I can offer my splendid parents is, at long last, an answer to the question, "When will you be finished?"

Finally, I wish to thank my husband, William Poteat, without whose love and encouragement this project would not have been completed. More important than his forbearance of the night exaltations and morning terrors provoked in me by the rigors of writing this book has been the sure knowledge that no matter what the outcome, his love, like the hound of heaven, would follow me still.

Walker Percy and the
Old Modern Age

Prologue

Only in man does the self miss itself, *fall* from itself. . . . Suppose I could hit on the right dosage and weld the broken self whole! What if man could reenter paradise, so to speak, and live there both as man and spirit, whole and intact man-spirit, as solid flesh as a speckled trout, a dappled thing, yet aware of itself as a self.
THOMAS MORE
in Walker Percy's *Love in the Ruins*

Why does man feel so sad in the twentieth century?
WALKER PERCY
"The Delta Factor"

IN *Love in the Ruins*, the third of Walker Percy's five novels, Thomas More, M.D., shows himself to be a highly astute diagnostician not only in respect to such straightforward ailments as swamp fever, large-bowel complaints, and migraine headaches but also in respect to those more subtle aberrations of the soul which issue in night exaltations, morning terrors, and generally inexplicable behavior—all of which afflict Dr. More. Percy, himself an M.D., proves an equally astute diagnostician when speaking in the first person in "The Delta Factor," first of the essays collected in *The Message in the Bottle*. The series of questions with which that essay begins directs our attention to the peculiar malaise afflicting man in the twentieth century. This malaise is evident in such odd circumstances as, for example, the fact that America's most beautiful city, San Francisco, has its highest suicide rate; the fact that war seems to be man's greatest pleasure; the fact that as Jean Paul Sartre sat in a café writing about the absurdity of human existence, he was very likely the happiest man in France; and finally, the general tendency of people to feel bad in good environments (*e.g.*, "suburban Short Hills, N. J. on an ordinary Wednesday afternoon") and good in bad environments (*e.g.*, "an old hotel on Key Largo during a hurricane").[1] Percy asks, "Why?"

The issue implicit in these examples is one common to both Percy-as-novelist and Percy-as-essayist. In each of the five novels, in the essays collected in *The Message in the Bottle*, and in those published singly, he directs his polemic again and again at the sundry insanities of the modern philosophic tradition rooted in Descartes. In particular, he takes aim at those tenets of the tradition which render problematic any coherent sense of the self or the person. Given the modes of argument available to the novelist and to the essayist respectively, he seeks to devise a cogent critique of the regnant Cartesian ontology, an ontology which severs soul from body, relegating the one to the company of angels and the other to that of the beasts.

It would be entirely accurate to say that there is nothing unique about this. Percy is not the first nor is he apt to be the last critic of thinkers whose chief intellectual progenitor is René Descartes. Two things, however, do distinguish his work in this area. First, Percy stands with those few (*e.g.*, Albert Camus) who have challenged the Cartesian tradition in two very different literary modes requiring a great range of imaginative and rhetorical talents as well as philosophical expertise. Second, the cogency of Percy's critique varies according to the mode in which he writes. While his polemical barbs are almost unfailingly on target in the novels, they often go astray in the essays. This is not to say that as an essayist Percy is either philosophically naïve or stylistically incompetent. Quite the contrary. The essays display a sophisticated grasp of complex philosophical and linguistic issues as well as a formidable array of stylistic and rhetorical skills. I do mean to suggest, however, that despite his obvious talents for writing expository prose (indeed, perhaps *because* of them), Percy's conceptual vision becomes progressively more blurred as his style and vocabulary become progressively less anecdotal or narrative and more analytical and abstract—hence, ever more tenuously anchored in the concrete particulars of persons in predicaments.

In the context of his "frontal assault" upon the Cartesian picture of the self, Percy exhibits a profound confusion vis-à-vis those very issues he addresses with such acumen in the more indirect polemic of the

---

1. Walker Percy, *The Message in the Bottle* (New York, 1975), 4.

novel. As his gaze wanders from persons in predicaments and fixes it-self with increasing tenacity upon "an explanatory theory of man," [2] Percy himself falls victim to the very incoherence of modern philoso-phy he intends to criticize. Consequently, he manages in the end to im-pale himself on the horns of the old Cartesian mind/body dilemma and fails to realize his own conceptual aspirations.

Percy's failure in this regard is, however, most illuminating. The phenomenon of novelist-poet donning the garb of critic-moralist-philosopher is no rarity. T. S. Eliot produced a substantial body of lit-erary and moral criticism. In aphorisms, forewords, and afterwords, and in sundry critical essays, W. H. Auden gave voice to a sensibility about the human condition that deserves to be called his "philosophy" and recognized as continuous with that embodied in his poetry. Graham Greene as well has written brilliant autobiographical and critical pieces alongside his novels and "entertainments." In none of these cases, however, does one so readily sense the profound in-congruity between novel or poem and essays which obtains between those of Percy—this due almost entirely to the fact that in their essays the former do not adopt with Percy's austerity either the agenda or the conceptual repertoire of the professional philosophic tradition.

It is at just this point that Percy's singularity in these respects af-fords us an opportunity to evaluate, side by side, the novel and the philosophical essay as instruments in the search for and articulation of a theory of man, and to observe in Walker Percy, himself an acute and clamant Everyman, the conflict of the philosophical dualisms against which he contends. This, then, is an essay in contemporary cultural criticism; that is to say, an essay in the peculiar perils of seeking to construct a radical philosophical anthropology by using the concep-tual tools of one's antagonists. Since Percy polemicizes in both his nov-els and essays, we can see not only the relative strengths of the two forms as rhetorical instruments in themselves. We can also see Percy, an astute critic and a serious man, struggling like Laocoön against the very weapons he has appropriated from his intellectual adversaries, only to have them turn in his hands against him.

In short, the rhetorical stance Percy adopts in relation to his subject

2. The phrase is Percy's and appears frequently in both "The Delta Factor" and in "A Theory of Language," *The Message in the Bottle*, 3–45, 298–330. What he means by "theory" in this connection is a point to which I shall return.

bears directly upon the felicity with which he carries out his critique of "the old modern age," the 300 years from the seventeenth century up to World War I, during which modernity assumed its characteristic bent and out of which arise all the puzzles, existential and philosophical, which dominate Percy's imagination. Moreover, this is the case not merely in the sense that one literary form provides a better "showcase" than another for the resolution of a philosophical problem, but rather in the substantive sense that a given literary form serves an author as an instrument for reflection. As such, it provides that author with intellectual and imaginative possibilities unavailable to him in any other mode. Further, by virtue of the very act of storytelling the novelist may disentangle himself from that "picture" of the human creature which lies at the heart of modernity.[3] Thus does he come to possess a singular power, the power to disclose the perils of living in a culture which understands itself to be centered in terms of an ontology which permits of no center.

THERE ARE two major presuppositions which inform these reflections. The first has to do with the claim that a literary form is an instrument for reflection and the second, with the claim that storytelling is a feat of knowing. To make the first claim is to suggest that a literary form is *intentional*. What does this mean? Bearing in mind that the word *etymology* derives from the Greek *etumon* meaning "the 'true' or literal sense of a word adjudged by its origin," I would suggest that the answer to this question lies in the "true or literal sense" of the words *intend* and *intentional*.[4]

The word *tend*—whence *intend* and *intentional*—has its origin in the Indo-European root *ten-*, meaning to stretch. The Greek cognate is *teniō*, meaning to stretch (by main force), to stretch to the uttermost. The Latin cognate is *tendere*, also meaning to stretch, to be stretched to (tend to). From *tendere* derives the compound and more immediate

---

3. I use the word *picture* here as Wittgenstein uses it in *Philosophical Investigations*, fragment #115: "A picture held us captive. And we could not get outside it, for it lay in our language and language seemed to repeat it to us inexorably." Ludwig Wittgenstein, *Philosophical Investigations*, trans. G. E. M. Anscombe (3rd ed.; New York, 1968), 48e.

4. Principal source for etymological data is Eric Partridge's *Origins: A Short Etymological Dictionary of Modern English* (4th ed.; New York, 1977).

antecedent of the English *intend, intendere,* meaning to stretch into or toward, to have the purpose or pretension of, to plan. Finally, the compound *intentus* becomes in medieval Latin *intentionalis,* yielding the English *intentional. Intentus* is itself an adjective meaning attentive and is thereby closely related to *attendere,* which means to stretch (especially the mind) toward, to pay attention to.[5]

The point I wish to emphasize here is that the radical *ten-* has to do not with stasis and repose but with motility and sentience—most simply the ordinary movement of stretching. Further—and this is a case in which the obvious is worth belaboring—stretching is not a random or haphazard movement as is, for example, the movement of certain subatomic particles in individual atoms. Rather, it is movement possessed of a particular bent, direction, orientation, or telos—*e.g.,* that of the one-celled amoeba stretching toward its food. This notion of purposeful movement becomes clearer and more refined in the cognates and compounds derived from the radical. As varied as these derivatives are in their meanings, the root they share is profoundly teleological and provides for each the basis of its own particular bent.

To claim then that a literary form is intentional is to claim that it *stretches* the mind and imagination of an author in such a way that by choosing to write in one mode rather than in another he chooses a particular orientation both to the world and to his own words. This orientation issues in a repertoire of logically homogeneous images, metaphors, analogies, and rhetorical strategies which are the earmarks of a singular pretension. To put it differently, when a writer chooses "to tell a story" rather than "to construct a philosophical argument," he chooses one "language game" over another, and the imaginative and rhetorical territory assumes a shape, color, and type of inhabitant quite unlike what it would assume in the opposite case. Hence, the choice of a literary form, a rhetorical stance, a "voice" is not a trivial matter. One cannot "say the same thing" in one as in another because

5. It is worth noting a few of the other compounds sharing the *ten-*root: *contendere,* to stretch, esp. oneself, with all one's strength; *extendere,* to stretch out, to stretch to the full, whence *to extend; ostendere,* to stretch in front of, toward, whence *ostensive; portendere,* to stretch before or into the future, to presage or predict, yielding in English 'to *portend*'; *pratendere,* to stretch forward, whence both *tender* and *tendon; tonos* (Greek), a stretching, hence a raising of the voice, a pitch or an accent, a measure or a meter, whence *tone, tonic, intone.*

one form *pretends*—*i.e.*, stretches forward—the writer in one way while another would pretend that same writer in some other way.[6]

Finally, it is important to note if only briefly at present that in positing this connection between literary forms and the notion of intentionality, at least one other major conceptual move has quietly been made—*i.e.*, an alliance has been suggested between two concepts commonly held to be logically heterogeneous, namely, reflection and action. How so? Think again for a moment of the radical *ten-* with its irreducible connection to the motile, the sentient, the teleological, and by implication, to the temporal—in short, to the realm of action. To go on and argue that a literary form is both intentional and a necessary tool for thinking about the world in a particular way is to bring into a common habitation with reflection those attendant concepts buried deep within the "true and literal sense" of *intend* and *intentional*. Such a common habitation would be unimaginable in terms of the Cartesian understanding of reflection based as it is upon the (supposed) mutual exclusivity of mind and body, thinking thing and extended thing.

The precise nature of this alliance between action, reflection, and intentionality will, I believe, prove to be the key to Percy's success as a storyteller and his relative failure as a philosopher. For the present suffice it to observe that in both novel and essay literary form serves Percy well as an instrument for reflection. The question is: How well suited is the instrument to the task at hand?

This question as to the suitability of instrument to task also bears upon the second major presupposition informing my thesis, and once again, etymology will be helpful in disclosing it. The word *epistemology* derives from the Greek *epistēmē*, knowledge, plus -*logia*, the science or study of a certain subject. *Epistēmē* is itself a compound derived from *epi-*, upon, plus *histēmē*, I place; hence, "a placing of

6. Once again, I am using a notion from Wittgenstein's *Philosophical Investigations*. What interests me in particular about his concept of a "language game" is that, according to Wittgenstein, each of the following would be a language game: an attorney's defense of a client before a judge and jury; a physician taking a medical history, conducting an examination, and making a diagnosis; and finally, a theologian lecturing on systematic theology. The point is that each of these activities has its own linguistic elements and "rules" such that lawyer, physician, and theologian in practice draw upon a fund of images, metaphors, and rhetorical devices which are the province of his respective "language game." Cf. Wittgenstein, fragments 51–96, pp. 25e–44e.

oneself in the position required for." Thus, according to its true and literal sense, knowledge and, by implication, all our feats of knowing require that we dwell in the world in a particular way. This is to say that our way of knowing and our way of being are congruent and cannot be separated from one another.

In his essay "Knowing and Being," Michael Polanyi makes this point though in rather different terms: "To this extent knowing is an indwelling: that is, a utilization of a framework for unfolding our understanding in accordance with the indications and standards imposed by the framework. . . . If an act of knowing affects our choice between alternative frameworks or modifies the framework in which we dwell, it involves a change in our way of being."[7] I take Polanyi to be using "framework" here in much the same way as I have been using "instrument for reflection" and believe his point apposite to my thesis in the following way: If we think of a literary form as an instrument for reflection, we might say of the person who uses that instrument that as thinker and knower he stands in a singular epistemological relation to what is known. That is, by telling a story, he "places himself in the position required for" thinking about and knowing about the world in a certain way. Now, I have made the claim that the very act of storytelling may free a writer from that infelicitous image of the person which has dominated Western culture since the seventeenth century and, moreover, that it affords him a particularly advantageous position from which to elucidate those infelicities. In light of the etymology of *epistēmē* and of Polanyi's remarks, I want to go on to claim that the act of storytelling is an act of knowing carried out within a given "framework," the choice of which works a change in the very being of the storyteller. This change is such that he "places himself in a new position," consequently disentangling himself from that old way of being which *necessarily* issues from an allegiance—however tacit—to the Cartesian "framework."

This is to argue, in short, that in telling a story an author assumes an epistemological and an ontological status different from that he would assume in, say, the writing of a philosophical essay. Exactly what that status is and how it differs from the latter case will become

7. Michael Polanyi, *Knowing and Being: Essays by Michael Polanyi*, ed. Marjorie Grene (Chicago, 1969), 134.

clear in this study of Percy's work. What will also become clear is why those forms of knowing and being that are the province of the story-teller provide the best conceptual tools for the task of "welding the broken self whole" and for answering the question "Why does man feel so sad in the twentieth century?"

This analysis does not, therefore, assume that Walker Percy is a superb novelist who happens, by the by, to write philosophical essays. It assumes, rather, that an intense animus for cultural criticism and polemic informs both activities. It also assumes that the brilliant success of the novelist, together with the *systematic* and therefore philosophically revealing confusion of the essayist, discloses the profound differences between the novel and the philosophical essay as instruments for reflection—a thing fascinating in itself and, even better, one full of implication for the very nature of modern cultural criticism to which Percy aspires.

I ℯ

"The Delta Factor"

OR, ON THE JOYS AND SORROWS OF BEING
WITHOUT A THEORY OF MAN

The reason why it may be wise to distrust the political judgements of scientists *qua* scientists is not primarily their lack of "character" . . . but pecisely the fact that they move in a world where speech has lost its power. And whatever men do or know or experience can make sense only to the extent that it can be spoken about.
HANNAH ARENDT
The Human Condition

That is why we despair. . . .
　　　　　　We are afraid
Of pain but more afraid of silence;
　for no nightmare
Of hostile objects could be as terrible as this Void.
This is the Abomination. This is the wrath of God.
W. H. AUDEN
For the Time Being: A Christmas Oratorio

The end of the age came when it dawned on man that he could not understand himself by the spirit of the age, which was informed by the spirit of abstraction, and that accordingly the spirit of the age could not address one single word to him as an individual self but could address him only as he resembled other selves.
　　Man did not lose his self in the modern age but rather became incommunicado, being able neither to speak for himself nor to be spoken to.
WALKER PERCY
"The Delta Factor"

A BASIC fact of life in the twentieth century is that we find ourselves hard pressed to say who we are and what we do. More particularly, ordinary discourse has little or no purchase when it comes to the "serious" business of modern science and technology, much of which is transacted in mathematical symbols and equations and all of which bears heavily upon contemporary life. So intimately is speech bound up with our sense of self that our ability to make sense of the world and of our place in it has, consequently, been severely eroded. Thus are men left to seek other ways to establish their own reality. One of the more poignant of these is the modern obsession with picture taking, a means by which, Percy observes, individuals may "prove despite their deepest suspicions to the contrary that they [are] not invisible." [1]

What is at stake in this cultural diminution of speech is no less than

1. Walker Percy, *The Message in the Bottle* (New York, 1975), 26. Subsequent references appear in the text in parentheses; *The Message in the Bottle* is abbreviated MB.

9

the single thing which clearly distinguishes man from all other creatures. Hence to take away a man's ability to speak and be spoken to is to deprive him of something profoundly and uniquely human. As Percy puts it, to render a man "incommunicado" is to make of him "a ghost at a feast," deprived of any ready means by which to appear in and make sense of the world of speech and action shared by other men. He is, in a word, out of this world. In "The Delta Factor," Percy takes seriously this irreducible connection between our ability to speak and be heard, on the one hand, and the singular joys and sorrows of being human on the other. With this as his starting point, he proposes that if we pay very careful attention to the actual phenomenon of speech we might be well on our way to understanding what is amiss with the lord of the earth and to discovering a cure for his malaise. Percy makes his intentions quite plain: "There is only one place to start: the place where man's singularity is there for all to see and cannot be called into question even in a new age in which everything else is in dispute. That singularity is language." And later: "This book [*The Message in the Bottle*] is about two things, man's strange behavior and man's strange gift of language, and about how understanding the latter might help in understanding the former" (MB, 7, 9).

Put with commendable economy, this is the thesis of *The Message in the Bottle* in general and of "The Delta Factor" in particular. Faced with the lack of any satisfactory theory of man—*i.e.*, one which will account for his alienation—Percy sets out to devise a new one fit for the new age whose spirit is not yet known. Since, he claims, everything except man's ability to speak is currently in dispute, this seems the logical if indeed not the only place to begin. *Homo loquens*, man the speaking animal; *Homo symbolificus*, man the symbol-monger: this will be his special province.

Percy is surely on the right track when he claims that the way a man uses language may tell us something about the way he thinks and knows and about why he acts as he does. Applied reflexively to "The Delta Factor," this thesis discloses a shrewd diagnosis of the modern malaise, the clarity of which accrues to the singular plexus of conceptual tools and language games Percy uses to present his argument. At once more problematic and more illuminating, however, his argument as to the probable causes and possible cure for that malaise is *least* clear and persuasive at those points at which he is preoccupied with theory per se as distinct from the speaking event in its existential context. As we shall see, these points are the very ones at which his rhetorical stance severs him from his grounding in the particular and the concrete, hence from his best conceptual instincts.

IN THE PROLOGUE to this essay, I suggested that Percy's conceptual vision is most clear when he focuses his attention upon persons in predicaments and significantly less so when he concentrates on devising an explanatory theory of man. Implicit in this assertion is the thesis that novels are "clear" in some way importantly different from that in which philosophical essays are "clear." With this in mind, two questions naturally arise: What do I mean by "clear" in this context? And, what sort of activity is it to devise a theory? Answering these questions will provide a convenient way to open up "The Delta Factor," and I shall begin with the second, my aim being to develop a model of clarity other than the one we have inherited from Descartes. From there I shall go on to show how this alternative model is embodied in "The Delta Factor" and issues in a picture of the human creature significantly different from its Cartesian counterpart. This point will in turn provide a basis upon which to evaluate the intentional character of the language games Percy practices in the essay.

If one looks for the etymology of *theory* in Eric Partridge's *Origins*,[2] he is directed to the entry for *theater*. This might come as a surprise to those of us schooled in the Enlightenment tradition and for whom *theory* is likely to be associated with things "scientific," "rational," "rigorous," "intellectual," and just plain serious. On the other hand, we might equally be inclined to associate *theater* with activities which, compared to either philosophy or science, are decidedly second-class, intellectually speaking—*e.g.*, "make-believe," "play," and that which is not "really" true. Our probable uneasiness notwithstanding, however, the fact is that *theory* is of the same family as the Greek *theatron*, or theater. *Theatron* is akin to *thea*, a sight, and to *theasthai*, to view, which is itself related to *thauma*, a thing compelling the gaze, and to *theōrein*, meaning to look at. The latter is the direct

2. All data on *theory* from Eric Partridge, *Origins: A Short Etymological Dictionary of Modern English* (4th ed.; New York, 1977), 710–11.

antecedent of the late Latin *theoria*, whence the English *theory*. *Theoria* means a looking, a seeing, an observing, or a contemplation, hence a speculation.

Three points must be emphasized about the etymology of *theory*. First, consider what is suggested by the kinship between *theory* and *theater*. To watch a theatrical performance one must necessarily be at some distance from the actors, preferably where he can view the entire stage at a glance. From this vantage point outside the sphere of action, he observes the progress of the tale which has its own internal coherence. For all of the fact that if the play is a good one the theatergoer may be deeply moved by what he sees on the stage, the pleasure he takes in his experience is contingent upon a posture of detachment, a status as observer rather than as participant.

Second, it is worth noting that theater is very much a public art form. A performance requires an audience however small and the play appears whole and intact to everyone. It is "out there in the world" and available to all without prejudice. This sense of something being "out there" for any who care to see it is evident not only in a commonsense account of theatergoing but also in the meaning of *theōrein*, to look at, and even more explicitly in the lineage of *theory*'s etymological cousin, *theorem*. The latter derives from *theōrein* via *theōrēma*, meaning a sight or an object of study.[3]

The third point follows closely upon the first two—i.e., both its connection with *theatron* and with *theōrein* suggest an alliance between *theory* and the sense of sight or, more properly, with metaphors drawn from the sense of sight. Theater is first, though of course not exclusively, a visual medium. Our sense of sight enables us to follow the action of the play and be engaged by it while at the same time keeping our distance. Also, it gives us the illusion of taking in that action "at a glance" or "in the instant." This alliance is even stronger in the direct line of descent from *theorein* to *theory*. There the dominance of the visual sense is plain: to have a theory about something is, most simply, to stand back and look at it.

---

3. There is another notion which issues from the public nature of theater, namely, that theatergoing is an importantly convivial enterprise. This point will be central in the development of an alternative model of clarity, one no less firmly rooted in the etymology of *theory*.

What then does this suggest about the activity of devising a theory? Or, more precisely, what might we logically infer from the etymology of *theory* as to the onto-epistemic posture of one who is bent upon devising a theory of man? Like a play, a theory is a moveable feast. It is incumbent upon the theorist no less than upon the playwright to devise a "picture" which has an internal coherence and veracity and which may be displayed before any number of audiences in any number of settings and, if the playwright or theorist is very skillful, before a great many generations. Unlike the playwright, however, the theorist (and I have in mind here and in what follows the one after no less than a theory of man himself) is not concerned with presenting a picture of particular characters in particular situations. Rather, his interest lies in devising a picture which has veracity for all characters in all situations—*i.e.*, a picture of men not as individual selves but as they resemble other selves (cf. MB, 26).

This distinction between the respective agendas of the playwright and the theorist is a very telling one as both are intent upon devising a presentation of reality. While these presentations are analogous in some important respects, the point at which they diverge is even more significant. The playwright seeks to devise a picture which, for all of the fact that it is viewed in public and from a distance, will nevertheless make sense because it touches the theatergoer at some point in his own history and situation. Thus is the sense of the play's being "out there in the world" mitigated. Further and more to the point, it is mitigated precisely to the degree that the internal coherence of the tale bears upon the singular predicament of each auditor. In constrast, the presumption of the theorist is that he might devise a picture the truth of which must be acknowledged by his audience quite apart from its members' respective histories and situations. Consequently, the sense that the theory exists "out there in the world" is not only unmitigated but is the *sine qua non* of its veracity. Indeed, if the truth of the theorist's propositions were thought to be in any way contingent upon such "personal" or "subjective" criteria, it would be rejected *ipso facto*.

This is a very slippery slope indeed, and my choice of the word *presumption* in this context is quite deliberate. In the two preceding paragraphs, I have had in mind the regnant model of *theory* and *theorizing* the bare bones of which Polanyi describes quite succinctly. According to this model, a theory is "something other than myself":

> A theory on which I rely is therefore objective knowledge insofar as it is not I, but the theory which is proved right or wrong when I use such knowledge. . . . A theory, moreover, cannot be led astray by my personal illusions. . . . It has a rigid, formal structure, on whose steadfastness I can depend whatever mood or desire may possess me. . . . Since the normal affirmations of a theory are un-affected by the state of the person accepting it, theories may be con-structed without regard to one's normal approach to experience.[4]

Theory, then, as we commonly think of it, bears the unmistakable imprimatur of the Cartesian framework. Our philosophical tradition has abstracted or *drawn out* of the "true and literal sense" of *theory* precisely those shades of meaning which accord with the Cartesian ac-count of thought. This account is, of course, heavily weighted in favor of the discarnate intellect seeking to know the world/object with per-fect lucidity through the offices of reason uncontaminated by experi-ence. This second-order account of what it is to think and, subse-quently, to have a theory about something is all a part of the language game which comes into play when Percy sets out to devise "an ex-planatory theory of man."

The very intention (or presumption) to devise such a theory consti-tutes the choice of a "framework" in Polanyi's sense of the word. When the theorist sets out to devise a theory of man, he indwells that intention in such a way that his understanding "unfolds in accordance with the indications and standards" imposed by it. In this case, the indications and standards of his framework are largely governed by the spirit of abstraction which afflicts modernity and which elicits a certain pretension from the thinker who relies on that spirit to inform his own conceptual agenda.

We might equally describe the theorist's presumption in another way using the idiom of Wittgenstein. To turn one's energies to devising a theory of man is to take up a particular "language game" governed by its own rules and providing the theorist a singular fund of linguistic elements with which to do his work. Accordingly, a certain "picture"

4. Michael Polanyi, *Personal Knowledge* (Chicago, 1958), 4.

of the human creature is implicated by that language game and embodied in those linguistic elements. In this case, the latter trade heavily in metaphors drawn from the sense of sight and from the activity of theatergoing in such a way as to emphasize the distance or disjunction between oneself and the object of one's attention. This distancing in turn renders the distinction between subject and object the superordinant category for thinking about the world, making that world (including one's own body) merely an object for speculation. This disposition finds its ultimate expression in Descartes' "*Cogito, ergo sum.*"

It is useful to remember in this connection that the word *abstract* derives from the Latin *tractāre*, meaning to draw violently or long or effortfully; and more immediately from *abstrahere*, to remove by pulling. The spirit of abstraction which informs Enlightenment thought does precisely this, drawing us away from the concrete particularities of our own mind-body, our own situation in the world, and toward some realm in which bodies have no place and minds swing free from all such "incumbrances." It is a realm in which language with its tenses and personal pronouns yields to the univocal symbols and equations of mathematics, which are grounded in neither time nor place and with which we may address no one by his proper name. This truly radical shift in human consciousness and aspiration is what Hannah Arendt has in mind when she argues that the earth is "the very quintessence of the human condition" and then traces the alienation of the modern world to our "twofold flight from the earth into the universe and from the world into the self." In their desire to know as the angels know, scientists have made this "twofold flight" with a vengeance. Consequently, they have been so thoroughly drawn out of this world that they are indeed "ghosts at a feast" and, as Arendt observes, their new world one in which "speech has lost its power."[5]

How does all this bear upon our understanding of clarity? Logically homogeneous with the spirit of abstraction is an obsession with theory, that moveable feast to be enjoyed by Anyone, Anyplace. These together comprise the regnant criterion for clarity, namely that to be clear something must be at least *in theory* fully explicable and subject to proofs of a mathematical or "scientific" sort. This is to say that anything which is subject to the understanding must be of the same

5. Hannah Arendt, *The Human Condition* (Chicago, 1958), 2, 6, 4.

logical order as mathematics; it must exhibit the same "certainty and self-evidence of [mathematics'] reasonings."[6] All else may be dismissed as philosophically trivial.

Perhaps the most striking feature of this model is that by allegedly eliminating the personal and the temporal from our feats of knowing it offers a haven of intellectual certainty in an otherwise uncertain universe. With characteristic acuity, Pascal recognized its powerful appeal: "Nothing stands still for us. This is our natural state and yet the state most contrary to our inclinations. We burn with desire to find a firm footing, an ultimate, lasting base on which to build a tower rising up to infinity."[7] Caught up as we are in the messy contingencies of everyday life, the possibility of building "an ultimate, lasting base" from which to launch ourselves into the world with relative safety is very seductive indeed. The difficulty arises only when we stop to consider the picture of the self implicated (literally, folded in) in such a scheme. In his Second Meditation, "Of the Nature of the Human Mind; and that it is Easier to Know than the Body," Descartes describes his body as "a machine made up of flesh and bones" and then goes on to suggest that his living flesh is not importantly different from that of a corpse. This rather unnerving comparison comes in the midst of his discussion of "thinking thing" (mind) and "extended thing" (body), and in the wake of both his proposition "*Cogito, ergo sum*" and his superordination of mathematical reasoning as the model for all knowing.[8] Together these dicta comprise the rudiments of the Cartesian framework, the Cartesian language game. Implicated therein is a picture of the self: reasoning intellect riven from corpselike body, aspiring to the certitude of clear and distinct ideas modeled upon the univocal meaning of a mathematical equation. This is the picture of the self funded by that spirit of abstraction and obsession with theory which issue in the Cartesian model of clarity. This is also the picture of the self which equates the personal with the "merely subjective" and so renders it philosophically trivial.

6. René Descartes, *Discourse on Method and The Meditations*, trans. F. E. Sutcliffe (Baltimore, 1968), 31.
7. Blaise Pascal, *Pensées*, trans. A. J. Krailsheimer (Baltimore, 1966), 92.
8. Descartes, *Discourse on Method and Meditations*. See especially Discourse #2, pp. 40–44, and Discourse #4, pp. 53–60.

As I progress in my argument, I shall refer many times to this Cartesian picture of the self as well as to its attendant concepts of abstraction and objectivity, a preoccupation with theory, the superordinance of the distinction between subject and object, and the epistemological framework all these comprise. However, before going on to develop an alternative model of clarity and, subsequently, an alternative picture of the self, I wish to underscore my reason for explicating these notions with some care early on. My purpose here has been to focus attention upon certain salient features of the Cartesian language game or framework, in particular, those which figure importantly in Percy's use of the philosophical essay as an instrument for reflection. The specific ways these features "work" for Percy I have yet to demonstrate and shall of course do so in due time. For the moment, however, my aim has been rather more modest, namely, to make as plain as possible the "indications and standards" of that framework according to which my evaluation of Percy will unfold. Part of that task lay in focusing upon the Cartesian model of clarity and the ontology and epistemology embodied in it. The next lies in proposing an alternative model, one which is equally at work for Percy and, I believe, more appropriate to his conceptual agenda.

In the prologue, I noted that Percy often uses anecdotes in his essays, making his point through the presentation of what one reviewer aptly calls "little dramas of ordinary experience."[9] "The Delta Factor" exhibits one of the most sustained and complex uses of this device in, for example, the series of rhetorical questions with which the essay begins, in the introduction of a very inquisitive Martian, and in the story of Helen Keller's great discovery at the well house in Tuscumbia, Alabama, in 1887. This strategy of presenting the reader with a particular character in a particular situation provides the germ of that alternative model of clarity we seek.

Two points made earlier are worth recalling here. First, one important difference between the playwright's way of presenting reality and that of the theorist is that the former does so by introducing his audience to characters with proper names who find themselves in a certain

9. Jonathan Culler, "Man the Symbol-Monger," *Yale Review*, LXV (Winter, 1976), 264.

predicament. The theorist, on the other hand, contrives to present certain propositions which his auditors may evaluate noncommittally, giving assent or rejecting them solely on the basis of their "reasonableness." In their respective ways, both playwright and theorist are in the business of thinking about the human creature, one in terms of the idiosyncracies of personal histories and the other in terms of truths abstracted from all personal histories. Second, the most striking feature of the Cartesian model of clarity is that by disregarding the role of the personal and the temporal in our feats of knowing, it appears to offer that "ultimate, lasting base," that certitude about reality we secretly desire. In effect, the Cartesian model allies reflection not with action and its attendant concepts of motility, sentience, and the temporal but rather with contemplation and its attendant concepts of stasis, repose, and the atemporal.

These two points together suggest a third. As an instrument for reflection, an alternative model of clarity must provide us with a new way to think about how we make sense of the world. Specifically, if it is to do the conceptual work we require—namely, to appropriate our incarnate condition as the *rightful* and *necessary* ground for all knowing—it must stretch our minds and imaginations not away from that condition but rather toward it. It must, in a word, restore the long-sundered connection between reason and experience, between "clear thinking" and "purposeful action." Such a model must embody an ontology and an epistemology which take seriously the fact that we are neither angels nor beasts *simpliciter* but akin to both and therefore, in Pascal's words, "incapable of certain knowledge or absolute ignorance." [10]

Where do we look for such an alternative? In discussing the salient differences between the playwright's and the theorist's respective ways of presenting reality, I suggested that the Cartesian understanding of theory and, subsequently, of clarity plucks from the fabric of all those concepts woven into the "true and literal sense" of *theory* certain threads which contribute to the presumption that a theory exists "out there in the world" quite apart from the personal backing of any individual. The result is the familiar second-order account of all our feats

10. Pascal, *Pensées*, 91, 94.

of knowing as logically of a piece with a mathematical equation. Present in this very etymology which contributes so heavily to the Cartesian model, however, are other threads which may be woven into quite a different picture.

The clue lies in the playwright's strategy of presenting his audience with persons in predicaments. Consider for a moment what constitutes the irreducible "stuff" of drama—persons, action, intention, conflict, resolution. In this, drama inhabits the same "logical neighborhood"[11] as the novel. The logical status of the concepts "person," "action," "intention, "conflict," and "resolution" is of the first order, and without them we would have neither art form. Consequently, if we regard the drama and the novel not as "mere" presentations of reality but rather as instruments with which to think about reality, then we might also say that these several concepts comprise the superordinant category for thinking about the world and as such determine the indications and standards according to which a picture of the self will unfold. This claim upon logical dominance is, of course, at odds with that implicit in the Cartesian *Cogito, ergo sum* in which the distinction between subject and object is superordinant and which issues in a picture of the self as a "thinking thing" set over against a world of "extended things."

Another way to put this would be to say that the language games of the drama and the novel share certain linguistic elements or "tokens."[12] This common fund is significant in that the bent or intention of these tokens ("person," "action," etc.) is toward the concrete, the active, and the incarnate as distinct from the abstract, the contemplative, and the discarnate. Hence, the "meaning" of the drama or novel resists abstraction; it cannot be *drawn out* since it is intractably bound up with those tokens which body it forth into the world and which are themselves firmly grounded in the particulars of persons acting and speaking.[13]

11. This useful image is from William Poteat's essay "Myths, Stories, History, Eschatology, and Action: Some Polanyian Meditations," in Thomas A. Langford and William H. Poteat (eds.), *Intellect and Hope: Essays in the Thought of Michael Polanyi* (Durham, N.C., 1968), 199–231. The phrase appears throughout.

12. *Ibid.*, 207–10.

13. This is not to say that the question "What does this story mean?" or "What is this story about?" may be answered only by retelling that story or by telling another one

This last idea points us directly to where the proverbial body lies. If indeed all this is buried deep in the roots of *theory*, then what we have here is the makings of a radically new account of what one is about when he sets out to devise a theory of man; or, we might equally say that we have in our hands a new and better instrument for reflection when the focus of that reflection is man himself. How so? If we set out to devise a theory of man according to the regnant understanding of *theory* then we must necessarily practice the Cartesian language game. Governed by the spirit of abstraction, the tokens of that language game (*e.g.*, "thinking thing," "extended thing," "certainty," "doubt," "*Cogito*") serve to reinforce rather than to dismantle a picture of the self in which mind and body, reflection and action are logically heterogeneous, to put it mildly. The most appropriate medium for a theory devised according to these lights is, I submit, the philosophical essay. Together with the tokens of the Cartesian language game, those rhetorical strategies which permit the author of such an essay to adopt a stance of objectivity and detachment in relation to his own argument (indeed, allowing him to disappear altogether) further the presumption that "serious" reflection may take place only to the extent that it is not contingent upon anyone's personal backing. To put it more concretely, the back row of the theater is ostensibly the best because the further away one is from the action the more detached he may be and so may have a clearer (and more distinct) idea of what is going on.

On the other hand, if we set out to devise a theory of man following the intimations suggested by the "backside" of *theory*'s true and literal sense, then we shall find ourselves practicing quite a different language game, the tokens of which point to *story* as the most fitting medium for our theory. Think of it this way: The logical neighborhood inhabited by the drama and the novel is not a flat plain but a region of hills and valleys encompassing certain topographical features which are in tension with one another. Specifically, watching a play or reading a

---

(though this might in fact be one way to answer). What I do mean to suggest is that to be intelligent, an answer to this query must bear a reflexive relation to the tale itself—*i.e.*, it must not discard the linguistic elements of the original in favor of some "better" (more theoretical or abstract) form of expression. Rather, it must maintain the bent or orientation of those original tokens, keeping in mind that the issue is not a function of the differential calculus but persons in predicaments.

novel requires a certain detachment while at the same time it elicits our engagement or presence by the skillful presentation of persons in predicaments. Absolutely essential to good dramatic or fictive writing, the tension between these two might equally be described as a tension between transcendence and immanence. Our appropriate detachment from events depicted in a play or novel permits us to transcend those events. Otherwise we might leap upon the stage to prevent Oedipus from blinding himself, or suffer a prolonged period of grief over the death of Little Nell. At the very same moment, however, the concreteness of the characters and situations unfolding before us commands our attention such that at least temporarily we are engaged by them no less than if they were exactly what they seemed—hence, the laughter unfailingly elicited from an audience by Falstaff's carryings on or the horror we feel when Huck Finn witnesses the slaughter of the feuding Grangerfords and Shepherdsons.

Herein lies the key to the appositeness of the drama or novel as a medium for a theory of man. The tension between transcendence and immanence embodied in these art forms is analogous to that embodied in ourselves *qua* selves. On the one hand, the transcendence we experience when watching a play or reading a novel is analogous to that we ascribe to the self, the "I," when we say it is not equal to the mere sum of its particulars. By virtue of our detachment, we are freed from the necessity of events depicted on the stage or in a book. Thus we are not bound to act in accordance with those events but maintain our freedom in relation to them. Similarly, as selves not univocally defined by the concrete particulars of our existence, we are greater than those particulars and so exercise freedom in relation to them as well.[14]

14. This freedom is not, of course, absolute. To make this claim would be to make Sartre's mistake and so fall back into the Cartesian trap. As William Barrett puts it, "In Sartre the individual disappears into the demonic and melodramatic possibility of his own freedom . . . [and] ends by becoming absence: no longer a person like you or me but the figment of his own abstract and impossible fantasy of liberty." Barrett, *The Illusion of Technique* (New York, 1978), xx. Let me illustrate my point with a rather crude example: If due to accident or disease a person has a leg amputated, then his life will be drastically changed and in some ways limited. Even so, this new and very unhappy circumstance does not determine or "equal" his self any more than did his prior condition as a two-legged creature. His *name* was not then "Two-Legged Man" nor does it now become "One-Legged Man." Rather it remains as it was, identifying him as an individual self, a part of whose story is now the fact that he walks on one leg instead of two.

On the other hand, the preeminence in both drama and novel of persons acting and speaking is equally the irreducible stuff of our own lives. Before we are anything else—doctor, lawyer, indian chief, or philosopher—we are speakers and actors living in time and in a plexus of other speakers and actors. From this, all knowing, all transcendence arises. Thus when we laugh or weep over Oedipus or Little Nell or Falstaff or Huck Finn, we do so for ourselves since what we see inescapably reminds us that we live and die not in a perfect world of pure reason and certain knowledge but in an imperfect one in which some weep while others rejoice, some go hungry while others feast, and some are lost while others are found. This is man's world, and in it he stands poised between the "two abysses of infinity and nothingness" and is to himself "the greatest prodigy in nature." [15]

Freedom from necessity embrangled in the limited, incarnate world of acting and speaking: this is the province of the human creature alone; it is the ground of his joy and equally that of his sorrow. To serve us well in this province, a theory of man must take seriously both aspects of our being, and not merely in an abstract way. Rather, it must itself embody these contraries, relying for its veracity not upon the tokens and pretensions of the Cartesian framework but upon those of storytelling. With its singular pretensions toward the concrete, the active, and the incarnate, the latter effectively recapitulates our experience of living, as Pascal says, midway between the infinitely great and the infinitely small and holding within us something of angel and beast alike. By thus bodying forth a picture of the self which embraces rather than ignores the ambiguities of our incarnate selves, storytelling provides the framework within which a new model of clarity unfolds.

If we think of storytelling as an instrument for reflection, then knowing is not of a piece with a mathematical equation nor is clarity equivalent to the presentation of clear and distinct ideas applicable to Anyone, Anyplace. Rather both are *situated* in the world of persons acting and speaking and cannot be abstracted from it. Accordingly, the clarity of a story hinges upon the degree to which it succeeds where the spirit of abstraction fails, namely, in addressing us as an individual self, not as we resemble other selves. This success depends

15. Pascal, *Pensées*, 91, 94.

upon two things: first, the skill with which the author practices the language game of his craft employing its tokens this way rather than that; and second, the relevance of the story to the reader's own personal predicament. As Percy puts it in his essay "The Message in the Bottle," the reader must stand in the way of hearing news else the import of the tale, no matter how artfully presented, simply will not exist for him.

These two points together indicate precisely where lies the most important difference between this understanding of clarity and the Cartesian one. As I have noted, the Cartesian model rests upon the presumption that any "clear and distinct idea" owes its clarity and distinctness to the fact that it stands out of time and on its own quite aloof from any person or setting. The alternative model briefly outlined here rests upon the contrary notion that clarity requires the personal backing and intent of at least two persons—author and reader or, if you will, speaker and hearer. It is, in a word, reflexive and convivial; it does not exist "in the instant" but requires time to unfold and persons to indwell and uphold it. This is to claim in part that the apprehension of the truth arises not from the reflections of the solitary intellect but rather in that space of appearance created when one person speaks and another listens and speaks in turn.[16] Further, it is to claim that the very nature of truth itself is not that it is "out there in the world" quietly awaiting discovery by the *Cogito*. Rather, truth is dramatic and agonistic and requires for its very existence the repeated affirmation of persons acting in concert and with intellectual passion, integrity, and commitment. Understood in this light, the apprehension of the truth becomes, in epistemological terms, the analogue of the political concept of the Greek polis. The polis is preeminently "the organization of the people as it arises out of acting and speaking together and its true space lies between people living together for this purpose no matter where they happen to be."[17] To thus ally the nature of the truth and by implication all our feats of knowing with a political con-

16. I am using the notion "space of appearance" as Arendt uses it—*i.e.*, "the space where I appear to others as others appear to me, where men exist not merely like other living or inanimate things but make their appearance explicitly." Arendt, *The Human Condition*, 198–99.
17. *Ibid.*, 198.

cept the heart of which is the speech and action of free men is to posit reality itself as that which cannot be apart from our lived mind-body speaking and acting with others; that which cannot be apart from the stuff of stories.

Conversely, to be deprived of this space of appearance and the apprehension of truth which accrues from it is to be deprived of no less than this very reality. Again, Arendt says it best: "To men, the reality of the world is guaranteed by the presence of others, by its appearing to all; 'for what appears to all, this we call Being,' and whatever lacks this appearance comes and passes away like a dream, ultimately and exclusively our own but without reality." [18] To be so deprived is to be silenced. It is to live as a ghost at a feast; to hear the awful quiet of Pascal's infinite spaces; to know in the poet's words, "the Abomination . . . the wrath of God."

BEFORE TURNING to the text of "The Delta Factor," one final point must be made. My development here of a way to think about theory, clarity, and truth other than according to the Cartesian model is no less a second-order account of our feats of knowing than is the seventeenth-century version. Hence, a claim to one model's superiority over the other cannot legitimately be made on the basis of the claim that one is "merely" second order while the other is something more "immediate." Rather, a claim to superiority can be made solely on the basis of how well these respective models "work"—*i.e.*, how well each explains or accounts for the ways we do in fact know and act. For instance, according to the Cartesian model, mathematics works precisely because it is *not* convivial but is rather a set of tautologies requiring the personal backing of absolutely no one. But is this really the case? Does mathematics not in fact work because we have all agreed that two plus two will always equal four? [19] While the answer is not so

18. *Ibid.*, 199. Arendt quotes Aristotle, *Nicomachean Ethics*, 1172b36ff.

19. Wittgenstein provides an excellent commentary on this question: "But mathematical truth is independent of whether human beings know it or not!—Certainly, the propositions 'Human beings believe that twice two is four' and 'Twice two is four' do not mean the same. The latter is a mathematical proposition; the other, if it makes sense at all, may perhaps mean: human beings have *arrived* at the mathematical proposition. The two propositions have entirely different *uses*.—But what would *this* mean: 'Even though everybody believed that twice two was five it would still be four'?—For what

simple as "2 + 2 = 4," my point remains: Mathematics is not merely a set of tautologies as the objectivist tradition would have us believe. Rather it is a "living science" depending for its value, intelligibility, and continuance upon the intellectual passion and commitment of individual persons.[20]

Another way to put this would be to say that the superior model is that which has the greater heuristic power. Using again the example of mathematics, an alternative model based upon storytelling is more likely to accommodate the actual practice of mathematics than vice versa. The Cartesian model can in no way account for either the simple or the complex joys of storytelling and story reading and so dismisses these activities as unworthy of the philosopher's attention. We might say, then, that the alternative model has the greater heuristic and interpretive power enabling us to think seriously about whole areas of human endeavor heretofore consigned to the no-man's land of the "unscientific"; or, even worse, condemned to play the part of Cinderella's sorry stepsisters trying to force their big feet into the dainty glass slipper of science.

Polanyi introduces a similar notion in discussing the intellectual power and appeal of Copernican astronomy. In particular, he seeks to explain the "true characteristics" of objectivity as distinct from the garbled version handed on by Descartes. He says in part:

> One may say, indeed, quite generally, that a theory we acclaim as rational in itself is thereby accredited with prophetic powers. We accept it in the hope of making contact with reality. . . . In this wholly indeterminate scope of its true implications lies the deepest sense in which objectivity is attributed to a scientific theory. . . . [Objectivity] is not a counsel of self-effacement, but the very reverse—a call to the Pygmalion in the mind of man.[21]

---

would it be like for everybody to believe that?—Well, I could imagine, for instance, that people had a different calculus, or a technique which we should not call 'calculating.' But would it be *wrong*? (Is a coronation *wrong*? To beings different from ourselves it might look extremely odd.)" Ludwig Wittgenstein, *Philosophical Investigations*, trans. G. E. M. Anscombe (New York, 1968), 226e–27e.

20. Polanyi, *Personal Knowledge*, 190. This understanding of mathematics is one Polanyi develops at length in *Personal Knowledge*, 184–93.

21. *Ibid.*, 5.

Of course, it would be ludicrous to claim that the proposals set forth in this essay are equal in scope to those of Copernicus. Still, Polanyi's point does bear upon mine and helps me to make it more clear: I do claim that storytelling provides a model of clarity and of truth which is presently indeterminate in scope. Moreover, this model has greater heuristic power and objectivity (Polanyi's sense) as a second-order account of knowing than does the Cartesian one. It will be the burden of what follows to show that these claims are well founded.[22]

IN AN INTERVIEW published in 1968, Percy was asked if it were true that his novels begin with a theme or idea. He answered, "I would rather say they start with a situation," and elaborated by saying that his chief concern lies with "a certain quality of consciousness put down in a certain place and then seeing what kind of reaction takes place between a character and his environment and the people he meets."[23] This remark equally describes Percy's strategy in the opening section of "The Delta Factor." The question with which the essay begins, "Why does man feel so sad in the twentieth century?," is but the first in a long series which fixes our attention quite firmly upon persons in predicaments and in particular upon situations singular to this postmodern age. For example:

> Why does man feel so bad in the very age when, more than in any other age, he has succeeded in satisfying his needs and making over the world for his own use?

22. If in response to these claims someone were to ask, "So are you simply saying that we cannot tell stories using mathematics? Isn't that obvious? And so what anyway?", my answer would be along this line: Yes, I am calling attention to this "obvious" fact. In addition, however, I am claiming that for all its obviousness, this fact is *not* philosophically trivial as it is commonly held to be. That stories do kinds of work for us which mathematics cannot is something our Cartesian culture simply overlooks or ignores. Specifically, the work they do is to enable us to think seriously about persons in predicaments—a logical impossibility using the conceptual tools and practicing the language game of mathematics. Nevertheless, many thinkers (including Percy) persist in their search for some "radical science" which will "explain" the human creature in all his idiosyncracies once and for all. Note: "radical science" is a phrase Percy uses in a very telling way in certain of his linguistic essays and in an important interview published in the Spring, 1981, volume of the *Georgia Review*. I shall return to this point in Chapters III and V.

23. Carlton Cremeens, "Walker Percy, the Man and the Novelist: An Interview," *Southern Review*, IV (Spring, 1968), 280.

Why do people often feel so bad in good environments that they prefer bad environments?

Why was it that when Franz Kafka would read aloud to his friends stories about the sadness and alienation of life in the twentieth century everyone would laugh until tears came?

Why do people driving around on beautiful Sunday afternoons like to see bloody automobile wrecks?

Why is the good life which men have achieved in the twentieth century so bad that only news of world catastrophes, assassinations, plane crashes, mass murders can divert one from the sadness of ordinary mornings?

Why does it make a man feel better to read a book about a man like himself feeling bad?

Why does no one find it remarkable that in most world cities today there are Jews but not one single Hittite, even though the Hittites had a great flourishing civilization while the Jews nearby were a weak and obscure people? . . .

Where are the Hittites? Show me one Hittite in New York City.

Why is it that the only time I ever saw my uncle happy during his entire life was the afternoon of December 7, 1941, when the Japanese bombed Pearl Harbor?

What would man do if war were outlawed? (MB, 3–7)

And so it goes for several pages. Such sharp, ironic questions and vignettes are hardly the sort of introduction we might expect to a topic so weighty as a theory of man and language. As one reviewer sagely observes, the opening of "The Delta Factor" is "neither a Skinnerian nor a Chomskian one," and, though the implication escapes the reviewer, therein hangs the tale.[24] Since Percy is neither a novice nor a fool, we can assume that "The Delta Factor" begins as it does not by accident nor to be merely entertaining, but rather that Percy opens his essay in a singular way appropriate to a singular intent. Let us look, then, at these first few pages to determine the conceptual end to which

24. Hugh Kenner, "On Man the Sad Talker," *National Review*, XXVII (September 12, 1975), 1002.

they are the rather unorthodox means and, more particularly, to take up the following question: If Percy gives us a clear and sympathetic picture of the modern malaise here (and I think he does), then how does that clarity issue from what at first seems a kind of scatter-gun approach to a large and complex dilemma? To put it differently, what language game is Percy practicing here and what are its tokens and pretensions whereby he conveys with great economy and concreteness the peculiar afflictions of modernity? The answer to this question will be consistent with the foregoing analysis of the concepts "theory" and "clarity" and with the thesis that Percy thinks most clearly when attending to persons in predicaments rather than to an explanatory theory of man.

To begin with, we might simply look at the dominant linguistic elements of this opening section. Over and over, in terse, epigrammatic style, we are confronted with images of profound dislocation. In this inside-out world, individuals think, feel, and behave in every way except that which by all reasoning they should. In short, they feel bad in good environments and good in bad environments. Percy conveys this dislocation not in a series of propositions about man or men but rather through concrete images of characters in situations, persons in predicaments—*e.g.*, his Uncle Will on Pearl Harbor day; the French and German veterans of Verdun returning to camp out in old shell holes and trenches; Jean Paul Sartre the happiest man in France even as he writes about the absurdity of human existence; the upper-middle-class New York commuter possessed of a loving family and all the creature comforts who often feels bad for reasons unknown; the difficulty of reading Shakespeare in a college classroom in contrast to the probable ease and appreciation with which it will be read by survivors of the next and last great war.

The effect of this strategy is twofold. First, by beginning his essay with such concrete, existential images, Percy firmly anchors his enterprise in the particulars of persons in predicaments. He might just as easily have anchored it in "Skinnerian or Chomskian" propositions abstracted from persons in predicaments and applicable to Anyone, Anyplace. In choosing to do otherwise, however, Percy establishes as the locus of his interest the everyday world of commuter trains, aging veterans, and college English classes. In effect, he invites us to pay attention to these seemingly trivial situations, implying that they are not trivial at all but give evidence of a profound unrest plaguing the human spirit in this most "advanced" age.

Second, Percy's tactic of presenting these images of dislocation in the form of questions serves an important heuristic function. Instead of presenting the reader with assertions to which he may say either "yes" or "no," Percy's repeated "Why . . . ?" invites a response of, "Now that you mention it, why indeed?" In this way, he elicits the reader's participation in the enterprise of, as Arendt would put it, simply thinking about what we are doing. This tactic makes a subtle but important difference in that as thinker and author Percy effectively allies himself with his reader, suggesting that our predicament is a common one best dealt with in a convivial way. Thus his rhetorical strategy quietly undercuts the regnant criteria for serious reflection insofar as those criteria hinge upon the solitary and perfectly lucid intellect arriving at clear and distinct ideas about nothing so trivial as the sadness of ordinary mornings.

On the basis of these observations, we can begin to answer the question as to Percy's language game here. Our first important clue is that the bent of his prose in these pages is indisputably toward the concrete, the active, and the incarnate and his attention clearly situated in the actual phenomena of persons acting and speaking. To put it succinctly, Percy, like Kierkegaard, asks the great simple question: What is it to be a man and to live and die? In particular, he wants to know what it is to be a man and to live and die in a world transformed by science; or more to the point, a world in which persons act as though the Cartesian picture of the self, perpetuated by science and ubiquitous in Western culture, were exhaustively true. In his attempt to answer this question, Percy stresses man's concreteness and the concreteness of his predicament. This is where he begins; this is what the opening section of "The Delta Factor" is about.[25]

Our second clue lies in the highly convivial mode in which Percy presents this concrete reality. Again like Kierkegaard, he does not seek

25. In an interview published in 1967, Percy says that the thing most attractive to him about Kierkegaard, Heidegger, Marcel, Sartre, and Camus is precisely their emphasis upon the concreteness of man's predicament. He then adds, "Perhaps a novel is the best way to render this concreteness." Ashley Brown, "An Interview with Walker Percy," *Shenandoah*, XVIII (Spring, 1967), 6.

to "edify," and indeed once remarked, "There is nothing worse than a novel which seeks to edify the reader."[26] This is significant in the present context in that there is something decidedly "unedifying" about the opening of "The Delta Factor." It gives us no answers. It does not offer a social program or a new psychology or a political platform which promises to cure us of night exaltations and morning terrors and make us rich and thin besides. Instead, what we get is an odd assortment of "little dramas" and more than a few vexing questions. This reluctance to edify is significant in that by eschewing the rhetorical posture of one who has arrived at some truth which he will presently dispense to his readers in a thoroughly edifying way, Percy also tacitly eschews the picture of reality implicated in such a posture, a reality having if at all then only incidentally to do with the space of appearance between two speakers. Rather, it discloses itself to and is most clearly apprehended by the solitary intellect. Too, its nature is presumably such that it readily lends itself to the formulation of clear and distinct ideas or, in the idiom closest to Percy's heart, to the formulation of explanatory theories. On the other hand, the rhetorical posture Percy does in fact adopt is logically of a piece with a reality vigorously resistant to intellectual formula. Instead, it is one replete with stops and starts, contraries and contingencies the apprehension of which rests not with the solitary intellect but rather in that space of appearance created at the juncture of "Why . . . ?" and "Now that you mention it, why indeed?"

This last point is most important as it discloses how radical is the implied epistemology of "The Delta Factor." Earlier I held that the apprehension of the truth arises in that space of appearance created when one person speaks and another listens and speaks in turn. This point issued from the prior argument that to serve us well a theory of man must rely for its veracity upon the tokens and pretensions of storytelling; and that accordingly the clarity of such a theory is irreducibly reflexive and convivial. It is precisely this "epistemological situation" which obtains in the opening pages of "The Delta Factor." Addressing himself to the unhappy fix we are in late in the twentieth

26. John Carr, "An Interview with Walker Percy," *Georgia Review*, XXV (Fall, 1971), 325.

century, Percy chooses the language game of the storyteller as his instrument of reflection. The intentionality of the tokens thereby at his
disposal is such that his prospective theory is firmly anchored in the
world of persons acting and speaking. By "anchored" I do not mean
merely "about" actors and speakers; Descartes' *Discourse* and *Meditations* are in an abstracted sort of way "about" actors and speakers.
Rather, Percy's theory is anchored in the important sense that his very
language at once constrains and empowers him to think about actors
and speakers in a way radically different from that of Descartes.

The constraint placed upon Percy by his choice of language game
lies in the necessity that he give logical dominance in his reflections to
the concepts "person," "action," "intention," "conflict," and "resolution." To put it differently, he is obliged to think of reality not in terms
of the lucid, discarnate *Cogito* and that which stands over against it
(which is to say everything other than itself) but rather in terms of the
reflexive, incarnate "I." This "I" discloses itself through word and
deed in the human world and yet is not nor ever can be exhaustively
disclosed or known either to itself or to others. It is rather implicated
in those words and deeds, an ontological "no see 'um." Again Arendt
puts the matter most succinctly: "The manifestation of who the
speaker and doer unexchangeably is, though it is plainly visible, re-
tains a curious intangibility that confounds all efforts toward un-
equivocal verbal expression."[27] By virtue of the constraints inherent in
the storyteller's language game, this complex union of the incarnate
with the intangible is the sole legitimate province of Percy's theorizing.
It must not only be his subject but also function as his epistemological
framework. As Polanyi might put it, he must attend *from* the incar-
nate/intangible self as well as attending *to* it.[28]

Conversely, the source of Percy's constraint is equally that of his
power. Clearly, his attack upon the Cartesianism ubiquitous in our
culture is not a case in which the best offense is to fight fire with fire.
Any attempt to "out-Descartes Descartes" is bound to fail because so
long as it trades in the tokens of Cartesianism it cannot free itself from

27. Arendt, *The Human Condition*, 181.
28. I have in mind here the from/to relation or the distinction between subsidiary
and focal awareness which Polanyi develops in Chapter 4, "Skills," *Personal Knowledge*, 49–65.

the suasions of those tokens, suasions which unobtrusively but inevitably uphold that picture of the self of which they are a part. The acuity of Percy's critique illustrates perfectly the fact that one cannot expose the fallacies of an argument while relying, however tacitly, upon the presuppositions of that argument. By coming to his subject armed with tokens of a bent contrary to those of the modern philosophic tradition, Percy enjoys a singularly good position from which to uncover the traps hidden by the seductively austere and "rigorous" objectivity of Descartes. As we shall see, however, he maintains this position only so long as he employs those tokens and continues in his practice of the storyteller's language game. To abandon them as he eventually does in favor of the tokens of Anyone, Anyplace is to forfeit the possibility of devising a theory of man situated in the human world and to slip back into the Cartesian framework and all that that entails.

For the present, however, let us stay with Percy's practice of the storyteller's language game and see how he fleshes out his initial skeletal diagnosis of our metaphysical ills. In general, the tone and rhetorical style of the first pages prevail in sections two through twelve, or until Percy turns his attention from "man's strange behavior" to the business of outlining an explanatory theory to account for that behavior. Thus, exclusive of the introduction, the essay falls into two parts roughly equal in length but decidedly different in tone and style. To evaluate this difference in light of the foregoing discussion, I shall focus upon the varying status of *theory* in Percy's argument. Specifically, I shall show that throughout the essay theory functions for Percy as a kind of conceptual lodestone but that an important change occurs in its epistemological value as he shifts his attention from persons in predicaments to an explanatory theory per se.

Beginning with section #2, Percy is at pains to do two things: to make his point that a coherent theory of man does not presently exist and to argue that the place to start in developing such a theory is language. As his argument unfolds, he is equally at pains to make clear that his interest in language is not the highly specialized interest of the professional linguist and makes the wry observation that "language is too important to be left to linguisticians" (MB, 10). Rather it is firmly situated in the routine business of ordinary people acting and speaking. He says at the beginning of section #3:

I don't even know what to call it, the object of this mild twenty-year obsession. If I say "language" that would be both accurate and misleading—misleading because it makes you think of words and different human languages rather than the people who utter them and the actual event in which language is uttered. So [*The Message in the Bottle*] is not about language but about the creatures who use it and what happens when they do. Since no other creature but man uses language, it is really an anthropology, a study of man doing the uniquely human thing. (MB, 11)

The effect of this declaration is to underscore the concreteness of Percy's enterprise, assuring us that his interest lies not in the language of Anyone, Anyplace—*i.e.*, language abstracted from specific speakers and events—but rather in that of particular persons in particular places acting and speaking with singular intent. Employing once again Polanyi's distinction between subsidiary and focal awareness, we might say that the modus operandi implicit in Percy's remark is that he will attend from language as such to the embodied self, that "no see 'um" in whose hands words are a potent tool for interpreting both self and other.

Seen in this light, Percy's interest in language might succinctly be described as broadly phenomenological and "situational" rather than narrowly analytic and theoretical (in the regnant sense of the word). Significantly, his choice of an example of a coherent (albeit presently bankrupt) theory of man complements this remark about his "mild obsession." In section #4, Percy states unequivocally his conviction that current theories of man are incoherent and then goes on to elaborate:

There does not presently exist, that is to say, a consensus view of man such as existed, for instance, in thirteenth-century Europe or seventeenth-century New England, or even in some rural communities in Georgia today. Prescinding from whether such a view is true or false, we are able to say it was a viable belief in the sense that it animated the culture and gave life its meaning. It was something men lived by even when they fell short of it and saw themselves as sinners. (MB, 18)

The "consensus view" he has in mind is, of course, the Judeo-

Christian one of man created in the image of God, possessed of an immortal soul and who lost his way in that "aboriginal catastrophe," the Fall; consequently, he became "capable of sin and . . . a pilgrim or seeker of his own salvation" (MB, 18).

Percy's choice of this particular example is most important and cannot be discounted as merely a telltale sign of his Roman Catholicism. At the heart of the gospel is the saving power of the Incarnation, that event by which, as St. Paul has it, God reconciled the world to himself. This is to say quite simply that the heart of the gospel is not a philosophical argument but a *story*—the story of *a* child born in *a* time and *a* place and of his teaching, suffering, death, and resurrection. According to this view, salvation lies in the indwelling of this story and there alone. As Percy puts it, "the clue and sign of man's salvation was to be found not in science or philosophy but in news of an actual, historical event involving a people, a person, and an institution" (MB, 18).

Consider for a moment what it means to claim not only that this "news" comprises a theory of man but a coherent theory at that. Clearly the word *theory* is doing uncommon duty there. First, what is the stuff of this theory? Obviously, it is not a clear and distinct idea which stands apart from any particular person, place, or time. On the contrary, its stuff is as Percy says, "a people, a person, and an institution." These are its principal tokens and their bent is decidedly toward the concrete, the active, and the incarnate. Second, what are the canons of acceptance for this theory? Acceptance has nothing to do with putatively noncommittal assent to a set of propositions open to empirical verification. Rather, acceptance requires that an individual hear in this story a personal address which speaks to his own predicament; that he take this address into his heart, indwelling it, "living by it"; and that, consequently, his life is imbued with a meaning and coherence it would otherwise lack. Third, if we were to override Percy's scruples and raise the issue of this theory's truth or falsity, what model of truth would be appropriate? According to the Cartesian model, what constitutes veridical knowledge is *only* that which appears whole and intact before the lucid, atemporal gaze of the philosopher. For his part, the philosopher allegedly stands in relation to the objects of his knowledge as God himself is imagined to stand with the world arrayed before him. In light of the two preceding points, this notion clearly will not do. Instead, the truth or falsity of the theory must be—to echo Percy's earlier remark—determined not by what it reveals about how we resemble other selves but by the acuity with which it addresses us as individual selves. This is to say that its veracity is not atemporal and impersonal, a once-and-for-all affair, but must be created anew each time the story is told. "For unto us a child is born." In the utterance of these words, there is created between speaker and hearer that space of appearance which is the dwelling place of reality. This theory must likewise make its home therein or else "pass away like a dream . . . without reality."

In a word, the Judeo-Christian story of sin and salvation exhibits neither the formal nor the logical properties we generally expect of a "serious" theory and cannot be deemed such according to the prevailing criteria or model. Instead, the criteria which are appropriate are those implicit in an alternative model of theory based upon storytelling. This story, perhaps more perfectly than any other, recognizes and interprets the ambiguities of our limited, incarnate, temporal selves. Indeed, not only does it recognize and interpret but, in the image of the Word made Flesh, consecrates as well. To put it rather colloquially, this story speaks to us where we live, accounting for our alienation and addressing the two issues which in Percy's view any cogent anthropology must address, namely, "the possibility of the perennial estrangement of man as part of the human condition and . . . the undeniable fact of the cultural estrangement of Western man in the twentieth century" (MB, 24). Therein lies its singular coherence and power *qua* theory.

It is important to note that this consensus view of the Judeo-Christian tradition is the only example Percy gives of a *coherent* theory of man. While I doubt he deliberately sets out to subvert our notion of what a theory should "look like," it is significant that, deliberate or not, his choice has just this effect. As we can see, Percy's use of the concept "theory" is when first introduced in "The Delta Factor" implicitly at odds with the regnant understanding of that concept while logically of a piece with the implied and quite radical epistemology of the essay's opening section. Further, by choosing as his example the "very cogent anthropology of Judeo-Christianity," Percy tacitly sets for himself certain criteria for coherence which if adhered to must issue in a theory similarly intent upon the concreteness and singularity of our mutual predicament. These two points together suggest that, at least early on, Percy's reflections are indeed guided by the intentionality not of the abstract tokens of Anyone, Anyplace but by the concrete ones of "an actual historical event involving a people, a person, and an institution."

There are, however, several snakes well hidden in the grass. Percy recognizes that, its coherence notwithstanding, the Judeo-Christian view of man is no longer the potent cultural force it once was. What we are left with is "a kind of attenuated legacy" evident in certain abstract notions like "God is love," "the truth shall make you free," "the sacredness of the individual," etc. This is one component of what Percy rather dryly refers to as "the conventional wisdom." The other is the profound impact upon our culture of the scientific revolution. In particular, he singles out that view of man which sees him as an organism in an environment not significantly different from other organisms in other environments. Put these two components together and what you have is not a coherent theory of man but one that is radically incoherent, its sundry parts going off in all directions "like Dr. Doolittle's pushmi-pullyu." The consequences are profound, ironic, and devastating:

> When the scientific component of the popular wisdom is dressed up in the attic finery of a Judeo-Christianity in which fewer and fewer people believe, and men try to understand themselves as organisms somehow endowed with mind and self and freedom and worth, one consequence is that these words are taken less and less seriously as the century wears on, and no one is even surprised at mid-century when more than fifty million people have been killed in Europe alone. In fact there is more talk than ever of the dignity of the individual. (MB, 21–22)

To put it with chilling succinctness, "The denizens of the age . . . are like men who live by reason during the day and at night dream bad dreams" (MB, 25).

At one point in his assessment of the status quo vis-à-vis a coherent theory of man Percy says quite simply, "Those who don't take this matter seriously forfeit the means of understanding themselves." This remark reflects quite accurately the intent of this part of "The Delta Factor." As Percy develops the critique of modern culture intimated in the question "Why does man feel so sad in the twentieth century?" the locus of his interest does not stray from what we might call the existential fallout of that confusion so deeply entrenched in the philosophical life of the West. Consistently resisting the temptation to extemporize on this or that Idea abstracted from any event or situation, his inquiry is carried forward by concrete images of persons making do when faced with the dilemmas and predicaments characteristic of life in the twentieth century. These range from the astronomer at work atop Mt. Palomar ("He is one of the lucky ones. It is his century and he is one of its princes. . . . But the question is, what manner of creature is he? Draw me a picture of Dr. Jekyll and a benign Mr. Hyde inhabiting the same skin.") to the nameless, faceless consumer living in the village below ("What happens to a man when he has to live his life in the twentieth century deprived of the sovereignty and lordship of science and art? . . . Does this consumer, the richest in history, suffer a kind of deprivation? What are the symptoms of the deprivation?") to the Unitarian minister ("good man that he is, who believes in all the good things of the old modern age, the ethics, the democratic values, the individual freedom, and all the rest") utterly at a loss to understand his son who wants out ("to him, anything, *anything*, is better than this fagged-out ethical deadweight of five thousand years of Judeo-Christianity") (MB, 21–23).

Percy does of course embroider these images and the ever-present questions with reflections and observations of a more general, analytic, even abstract sort. The important point, however, is that he never loses sight of his individual human subject, idiosyncratic in his disposition and intractable in his perversities benign and otherwise. All remarks are made in the service of speaking to and about this individual self and his singular predicament. Consequently, those passages in which Percy is not preoccupied with a specific "character" but is rather drawing some inference or making some observation about modernity as a whole—those passages are no less imbued with a keen and lively sense of the everyday world in which the speech and action (and craziness) of ordinary folk *matter* and from which the wholesale political and philosophical insanities of modern culture cannot be divorced. The passage below which follows upon Percy's point that the notion of the Fall presents a "stumbling block" to modern scientists and humanists alike provides a good case in point:

> So the scientists and humanists got rid of the Fall and reentered Eden, where scientists know like the angels and laymen prosper in good environments, and ethical democracies progress through education. But in so doing they somehow deprived themselves of the means of understanding and averting the dread catastrophies which were to overtake Eden and of dealing with those perverse and ungrateful beneficiaries of science and ethics who preferred to eat lotus like the Laodiceans or roam the dark and violent world like Ishmael and Cain.
>
> Then Eden turned into the twentieth century. (MB, 24)

Such is our predicament and Percy's assessment of it. By abjuring the infelicitous tokens and conceptual tools of the Cartesian framework and by keeping the image of persons in predicaments firmly in hand, his diagnosis of our sundry ills is vivid, on the mark, and polemically potent. What then are we to do about this unhappy state of affairs? How do we begin to rethink the way we think about ourselves? Percy is determined not to repeat the mistake of certain modern poets and artists who in his view "attacked the spirit of the age [but] had nothing to offer in its stead" (MB, 26). It is at just this point in his argument that a subtle and complex shift occurs in the apparent way he thinks about his project. Once again his use of the concept "theory" will be our guide through this uncharted territory.

First, we must backtrack a little. Near the end of section #2, Percy describes the theory of man he will soon propose as "the sort of crude guess a visitor from Mars might make if he landed on earth and spent a year observing man and beasts." Thus are we introduced to "the Martian." The special gift of this benign extraterrestrial visitor is that because he is an outsider he *can* see the proverbial forest for the trees. His special importance for our purposes is that Percy identifies himself with this creature:

As a nonpsychologist, a nonanthropologist, a nontheologian, a nonethologist—in fact as nothing more than a novelist—I qualify through my ignorance as a terrestrial Martian. Since I am only a novelist, a somewhat estranged and detached person whose business it is to see things and people as if he had never seen them before, it is possible for me not only to observe people as data but to observe scientists observing people as data—in short, to take a Martian view. (MB, 11)[29]

The image of the Martian and the notion of "taking a Martian view" are important tokens in the case Percy makes for developing a theory of man which takes as its starting point the fact that man is a symbol-monger. When the Martian arrives on earth having studied up on the biology, physiology, and psychology of his hosts, he is astonished to find that "earthlings *talk all the time* or otherwise traffic in symbols . . . while the other creatures—more than two million species—*say not a word*" (MB, 12–13) The Martian finds this passing strange. Even stranger is the fact that while linguists, semanticists, psychologists, and the like can tell him much about learning theory, stimulus-response theory, and transformational grammar, no one seems to take much interest in the very ordinary *event* of speaking and being understood. When he asks the obvious question, "What happens when people talk, when one person names something and says a sentence about something and another person understands him?," he gets at best an evasive answer and a copy of *The Naked Ape*. So the Martian concludes that something important has been overlooked here, something which might provide a clue to "the oldest and most vexed question of all, the nature of man" (MB, 16).

So far so good. The Martian conceit serves Percy well in making the point that, for all its sophistication and high-toned specialties, modern science simply cannot accommodate certain important aspects of human life, since anything not fitting into one or another narrowly defined area of expertise is lost, falling through the cracks between scientific disciplines. Further, Percy is right on target when he suggests that

29. Percy is obviously being ironic when he refers to himself as "nothing more than a novelist . . . only a novelist." His irony is well placed, however, in that according to the regnant intellectual hierarchy which places science above art, the novelist is just that— "*only* a novelist"—when it comes to serious reflection.

this difficulty can be surmounted only by approaching it with new conceptual tools having a heuristic power greater than those governing the practice of modern science. Implicated in the Martian conceit is the notion that those who indwell the Cartesian framework are oriented in such a way that, try as they might, they will be unable to see man as other than a creature who can "in theory" be exhaustively known (if only we had better technology, a more sophisticated computer, just the right experiment, etc.).

We might conclude, then, that "taking a Martian view" is just what is called for. More particularly, we might conclude that by virtue of practicing a language game other than that of modern science, Martian-novelist-Percy has just the perspective and appropriate detachment to see things afresh. The key here is "*appropriate* detachment." Earlier in discussing the etymological link between *theory* and *theater*, I suggested that the regnant understanding of theory draws upon the sense of detachment and objectivity necessary to enjoy a theatrical performance at the exclusion of the equally important sense in which the theatergoer must be present to and participate in the events on stage. With this point in mind, the case can now be made that the detachment of Percy's Martian has the potential for leading his reflections astray in *just this way*. That is, by focusing upon the Martian's detachment as his chief virtue, Percy may move in either of two directions. The first is that suggested in the preceding paragraph; namely, he may detach himself from the regnant ways of theorizing and go on to develop a new framework, a new language game with which to articulate the nature of man. The second is that which necessarily follows upon staying with the reigning Cartesian framework. In that context, the notion of detachment is synonymous with the position assumed by the discarnate, godlike philosopher in relation to the objects of his knowledge. If Martian-novelist-Percy moves in this direction, his reflections pretended by the tokens which will readily and inevitably come to hand, then it will be very difficult indeed to develop a theory significantly different from that which sees man as "a 'mind' somehow inhabiting a 'body,' neither knowing what to do with the other, a lonesome ghost in an abused machine" (MB, 44). It will be the business of the remainder of this chapter to show that this is in fact what happens.

JUST BEFORE TURNING to the Helen Keller phenomenon, Percy makes the following observation:

> The truth is that man's capacity for symbol-mongering in general and language in particular is so intimately part and parcel of his being human, of his perceiving and knowing, of his very consciousness itself, that it is all but impossible for him to focus on the magic prism through which he sees everything else.
>
> In order to see it one must be either a Martian or, if an earthling, sufficiently detached, marooned, bemused, wounded, crazy, one-eyed, and lucky enough to become a Martian for a second and catch a glimpse of it. (MB, 29)

To focus on the magic prism through which man sees everything else: this is the goal toward which Percy has been moving and of which he believes himself to be on the threshold. The vehicle which will carry him over the threshold is the story of Helen Keller's dramatic breakthrough at the well house, the moment when as she reports in her autobiography, "I knew then that 'w-a-t-e-r' meant the wonderful cool something that was flowing over my hand. That living word awakened my soul, gave it light, hope, joy, set it free" (quoted in MB, 35). Percy believes this brief incident holds the key to understanding what it means to be *Homo loquens*, *Homo symbolificus*: "For a long time I believed and I still believe that if one had an inkling of what happened in the well house in Alabama in the space of a few minutes, one would know more about the *phenomenon* of language and about man himself than is contained in all the works of behaviorists, linguists, and German philosophers" (MB, 35−36).

This is an extravagant claim and requires careful scrutiny. First, it is useful to note what Percy regards as the shortcomings of the two major schools of thought on language, the behaviorist (Skinner, Malinowski) and the German idealist (Kant, Cassirer). He applauds the behaviorist model for being "all a model should be . . . simple, elegant, fruitful," but regrets its inability to account for certain sorts of linguistic events—naming, for example, or storytelling. Percy credits the German idealists with paying serious attention to symbol, idea, word, transcendental forms, and the like but notes that in the process "the great wide world gradually vanishes into Kant's unknowable noumenon." In brief, he observes, "American behaviorists kept solid hold on the world of things and creatures yet couldn't fit the symbol into it. German idealists kept the word as internal form, logos, and let the world get away. From Kant to Cassirer, man became ever more securely locked up inside his own head" (MB, 33).

What is conspicuous by its absence from Percy's critique is any mention of the fact that both the behaviorist and the idealist schools are branches of the modern philosophical tree rooted in Descartes and the Enlightenment and that the constraints accordingly placed upon them are the source of their respective shortcomings. Clearly, it is beyond the scope of this essay to offer a detailed analyis of the conceptual debt owed Descartes by either behaviorists or idealists. It would be neither inappropriate nor controversial to observe, however, that each, in ways obviously different from the other, appropriates Descartes' fundamental distinction between "thinking thing" and "extended thing" and his conception of truth modeled upon the veracity of a mathematical equation, and makes of them the basis for its own putatively new way of thinking about reality.

This point is most important, as it perfectly illustrates the ubiquity in our culture of a certain repertoire of concepts, a certain set of philosophical dispositions, and the extraordinary difficulty of breaking free from them. It might be argued, of course, that by simply recognizing the shortcomings of the behaviorist and idealist schools Percy does quite enough to distance himself from the tradition of which they are a part. This is not the case, however, and it is not the case because it is not sufficiently radical. In effect, Percy criticizes these two schools of thought only insofar as they commit a sin of *omission*—i.e., their respective failures allegedly lie in what they leave out, not in where they started from. If Percy were correct, then all that would need be done would be to rectify these sundry omissions, leaving the original impetus for them unreflected and untouched.

The nature and significance of Percy's oversight here becomes more clear when we recall how he describes what he hopes to do in the essay's final pages: "to focus on the magic prism through which [man] sees everything else." Consider carefully the implications of this image. To accomplish this end would require that Percy assume the godlike detachment from actors and speakers of the Cartesian philosopher. The fact that he aspires to a mere "glimpse" of the language-prism does not mitigate the implication that such perfect detachment and lucidity are *theoretically* possible; nor does it mitigate the implication that man may be entirely transparent to himself. While very congenial to that tradition Percy supposedly abjures, both of these propositions are antithetical to the implied epistemology and criteria for a coherent theory which inform the introduction and first major portion of "The Delta Factor." The fact that this apparent shift occurs just as he begins to lay out his own theory suggests that the epistemological value of the concept "theory" has indeed changed. In particular, it suggests that Percy's criteria for devising a coherent theory have shifted from those implicated in the Judeo-Christian view of man to something much more in keeping with the regnant model of theory.

For further confirmation that this is indeed the case, we need not look far. On the heels of his critique of the behaviorist and idealist schools, Percy openly declares his own sympathies:

> My instincts, I confess, were on the side of the scientists in general and in particular on the side of the hardheaded empiricism of American behavioral scientists. . . . Was it possible, I wondered, to preserve the objective stance of the psychologist, which always seemed so right and valuable to me, which assumes there are real things and events happening, and to make some sense out of what happens when people talk and other people listen and understand or misunderstand? (MB, 33–34)

With this declaration, Percy makes two important conceptual moves. First, he implies that with respect to this complex issue there are two "sides" roughly analogous to the behaviorist and idealist schools and that one must choose between them. There is no mention or even hint that some third alternative exists quite apart from these two. Second, having delineated the two sides, Percy casts his lot with the former. To be sure, he does so with some reservations.[30] These notwithstanding,

30. In particular, Percy cites Chomsky's review of Skinner's *Verbal Behavior* as basically correct in its analysis of stimulus-response theory as being quite inadequate when applied to language.

however, he embraces wholeheartedly the fundamental predisposition of the behaviorist, namely, what counts as veridical knowledge about men no less than beasts must be grounded in the "objective" evaluation of certain neurophysiological phenomena, and that due to his special gift for detachment, the behavioral scientist enjoys a privileged position from which to make this evaluation.

These two points together uphold my earlier one vis-à-vis Percy's critique of the behaviorists and idealists. The real problem, as he sees it, lies not in the behaviorist model as such but rather in certain particulars of its application. Therefore, the solution must lie in refining and improving that model. Indeed, so convinced is he of the fundamental correctness of this approach as to say that, even without refinement, the behaviorist model is entirely adequate when applied to "the right kind of [human] behavior" (MB, 31).[31] Is it? I think not. The trouble with this equivocation is that to concede the model's rightness in this or that instance is also tacitly to concede the rightness of its basic premises and their efficacy as an instrument for reflection about the nature of man.

To put the matter concisely, it seems that, in his effort to rescue from the angelism of the idealists the ordinary world in which persons speak and act together, Percy turns for his model to the other side of the same coin, the bestialism of the behaviorists. The full import of this move becomes apparent when he offers his own "crude Martian's guess" of a theory in which the implied criteria for coherence is heavily behavioristic. Very briefly, Percy's theory is this: Taking Helen Keller's discovery at the well house as the paradigm for every person's learning that things have names (in her case, the process is telescoped into a brief moment), Percy concludes that this event is "a nonlinear, nonenergic natural phenomenon (that is to say, a natural phenomenon in which energy exchanges account for some but not all of what happens)" (MB, 39). Further, he concludes that the three "elements" involved in this event—Helen, *water* (the word), and water (the liquid)—comprise an irreducible triangle analogous to Charles Peirce's concept of "thirdness" and might be diagrammed as follows:

31. The example he cites is Malinowski's of Trobriand fishermen.

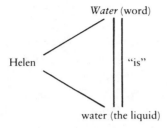

Water (word)

Helen   "is"

water (the liquid)

Finally, Percy goes on to suggest that this "Delta phenomenon" is nothing less than "the ultimate and elemental unit not only of language but of the very condition of awakening human intelligence and consciousness" (MB, 40) and as such, might be the key to understanding man's very strange behavior.

Now let us consider this theory more closely. What are its chief tokens and what may we infer as to the conceptual framework out of which it arises? The first thing to remark is Percy's penchant for drawing diagrams. In particular, it is significant that his first step in trying to understand Helen's breakthrough is to draw diagrams, "behaviorist models, showing the usual arrows" just as his "hardheaded" medical school professor had taught him. "After all," he adds, "the arrows were there." The extent of Percy's tacit commitment to behaviorist theory shows itself quite clearly here. Not only does he immediately turn to it when confronted with this puzzle but, even more important, he stays with it, failing to realize that its inadequacies are not trivial ones subject to repair but are truly fundamental and radical. Perhaps the most telling remark in this connection comes in the context of distinguishing the nature of his own interest in "what happened inside Helen's head" from that of the neuroanatomist. While the latter would want to know what synapses snapped when, Percy wants to know "what sort of thing happened" and then, as if the classic, Cartesian inside-the-head image were not damaging enough, goes on to say, "Accordingly, I kept thinking about Helen's breakthrough and drew dozens of diagrams, triangles, arrows, dotted lines, nerve nets linking portions of the sensory cortex" (MB, 37). In short, he continues to tinker with the behaviorist model on the implicit assumption that just the right diagram will deliver up to him that glimpse of the magic prism he seeks.

What exactly is it about this model which exerts such a powerful pull upon Percy's imagination at precisely this juncture in his reflections? The answer, I believe, is implicated in the passages remarked above and comes even closer to the surface elsewhere. It has to do with Percy's use of the notion "real." Remember that implicit in the regnant understanding of theory is the thesis that that which is "real" and "true" is logically of a piece with a mathematical equation and subject to similar proofs. Remember too that theory serves as a kind of conceptual lodestone for Percy throughout "The Delta Factor" but that its epistemological value changes significantly when he focuses upon a theory per se of his own. These two points now suggest a third. What seems to count for Percy as real and therefore fit to be an ingredient in his theory is that which can be diagrammed, looked at, measured; or, to put it another way, that which would satisfy the "hardheadedness" of his medical school professors whose preoccupation with "the mechanism of disease," he admits elsewhere, "amounted almost to behaviorism." [32] This is not to say that he expects to depict exhaustively the "mechanism" of Helen's breakthrough but rather that the reality of that breakthrough is nevertheless of the same logical order as something which is open to such depiction: "What dawned on me was that what happened between Helen and Miss Sullivan and water and the word was 'real' enough all right, no matter what Ogden and Richards said, as real as any S-R sequence, as real as H_2SO_4 reacting with NaOH, but *what happened could not be drawn with arrows*" (MB, 39).[33]

On the basis of this passage alone—given its despair of the efficacy of arrows—we might be tempted to think that Percy is at the eleventh hour about to cast off the behaviorist model. Unhappily, this is not the case. First, consider the weight of the phrase "as real as." In effect, Percy claims philosophical significance for "what happened" insofar

32. Quoted by John Carr, "Interview," 320. Percy goes on to say, significantly, "I realized that when you apply [the scientific method] to man, you stop short at the very point where it matters to man." *Ibid.*, 321.

33. Earlier Percy rejects Ogden's and Richards' "pseudo-triangle" as it fails to account for the "real relation" between the word *water* and the liquid. According to their scheme, it would be "an unreal imputed relation" and, Percy complains, could not be drawn on the blackboard (MB, 36–37).

as that event satisfies the same "hardheaded" criteria for the real satisfied by a stimulus-response relation (Trobriand fishermen fleeing a shark perhaps?) or a stable, predictable chemical reaction. He later reinforces this notion when he says of his irreducible triangle, "Using the concept of the Delta phenomenon . . . mightn't one even begin to understand the manifold woes, predicaments, and estrangements of man—and the delights and savorings and homecomings—as nothing more nor less than the variables of the Delta phenomenon *just as* responses, reinforcements, rewards, and such are the variables of stimulus-response phenomena?" (MB, 41). Again the implication is clear. Percy's depiction of Helen Keller's breakthrough stands in a logical continuum with Pavlov's and Skinner's depictions of their respective dogs and pigeons.

Second, we have to look ahead but one page to discover that while Percy does indeed abandon arrows, he does not abandon diagrams altogether. The reason he drops arrows from his scheme is in itself most interesting.

> The arrows tell part of the story but not the breakthrough. What seems to have lain at the heart of the breakthrough, what in fact *was* the breakthrough, was the fact that somehow the old chain of causal relations, the energy exchanges which had held good from the earliest collision of hydrogen atoms to the responses of amoeba and dogs and chimps, the ancient circuit of causes, my troop of arrows, had been shortcircuited. (MB, 38)

Consider carefully what Percy is saying here. The essence of Helen's breakthrough (and presumably that of *Homo sapiens* as a species) is that it "short circuits" certain "causal relations" so that the arrows which represented them are no longer necessary. Therefore, it is not that the arrows were "wrong"; rather, it is that they have been superseded by a kind of instantaneous shorthand—a "nonlinear, non-energic natural phenomenon"—to be represented by an arrowless triangle.

Percy seems to think that by getting rid of the arrows and making his triangle "irreducible" he avoids the behaviorist's reduction of any action to merely a set of causal relations. Arrows or the absence of them notwithstanding, however, Percy's surgery upon the behaviorist's triangle is not so radical as he believes. The basic fact remains: His "explanatory theory" rests upon a very considerable feat of abstraction. Specifically, he has abstracted or *drawn out* from a complex situation three "elements"—Helen, the word *water*, and water.[34] Notice that Helen is no longer a girl or a person; she has been magically transformed into an "element" and shares this dubious distinction with a certain word and a certain liquid. This is to say that suddenly Helen Keller, complex embodied self enjoying a plexus of relations with other equally complex selves, is logically neither more nor less than a word or a liquid and accordingly occupies one undistinguished corner of a static, one-dimensional, atemporal geometric figure. This point is most important, for it gives the lie to Percy's insistence that his theory, his "Delta phenomenon," plumbs that "something more" than causal relations which lies at the heart of Helen's discovery. Rather, Helen Keller's metamorphosis from person to "element" places his theory firmly in the tradition which views man as but an organism not significantly different from other organisms. To put it more vividly, her metamorphosis is logically of a piece with Descartes' remark that his living flesh is not importantly different from that of a corpse.

A second and equally important point must be made here about the three "elements" in Percy's triangle, namely, that Helen stands absolutely alone with her word and her water. Not even Annie Sullivan has a place in this scheme. In effect, by Percy's account, Helen's breakthrough is in no way convivial. Hence, her discovery of the liberating truth that things have names is allegedly the work of a solitary intellect and occurs quite apart from that space of appearance which in fact must have existed between the child and her gifted teacher as the *conditio sine qua non* of her learning anything at all. To claim that Helen could make such a discovery "in her head," her relationship with Miss Sullivan only incidental to the process, is to claim allegiance to a concept of the truth fashioned after the veracity and proofs of a mathematical equation and arrived at by the discarnate, godlike intellect of the philosopher.

Perhaps more than anything else, the one-dimensional, atemporal character of Percy's triangle, coupled with Helen's solitariness in it, re-

---

34. "Elements" is Percy's word and he uses it in this connection several times.

veals the essential poverty of the "Delta phenomenon" as an instrument for reflection. It is not, after all, importantly different from those models he rejects as "broken down." It does not, as he claims, provide a new way of thinking about language and the human condition. Why? Because in the end, Percy fails to build upon the radical conception of theory implicit in his diagnosis of our present cultural ills. Instead, when the time comes to propose a cure, he falls back upon the tokens and pretensions of behaviorism—which is to say upon the tokens and pretensions of one major branch of the Cartesian tree. The profundity and the irony of Percy's confusion in this matter must come home to us when he observes apropos of the behaviorist stimulus-response model: "When a model ceases to illumine and order or even to fit the case, and when the time comes that you're spending more time tinkering with the model to make it work than taking a good hard look at what's happening, it's time to look for another model" (MB, 32). If Percy simply paid attention to his own words and followed the criteria for a coherent theory implicit in his earlier remarks, then he might avoid the conceptual mess we find him in at the close of "The Delta Factor." The fact that he does not escape attests to the potency and ubiquity in our culture—indeed, in our very language—of certain concepts, images, metaphors, and analogies; to the ubiquity and power, in short, of a certain framework out of which arise some very infelicitous ways of thinking about ourselves and others.

EARLIER, I suggested that to try to expose the fallacies of Descartes' philosophy by beating him at his own game is a hopeless enterprise. This is precisely what Percy attempts when he turns his attention from persons in predicaments to "a nonlinear, nonenergic natural phenomenon." In so doing, he effectively sunders himself from his own roots in the human world of actors and speakers and, from that point forward, is no longer constrained to give logical dominance in his reflections to the concepts "person," "action," "intention," "conflict," and "resolution." Instead, newly constrained by a framework governed by the spirit of abstraction, he speaks neither to nor about individual selves but bends his energy toward devising an explanatory theory, a moveable feast, which may accommodate willy nilly Anyone, Anyplace. Percy's apparent assumption is that for his theory to be really "serious," he must abandon story or narrative as its medium in favor of the presumably more austere, rigorous, and therefore more veridical medium of abstract philosophical argument. This unfortunate prejudice on his part bears witness to the persistent power of certain epistemological values born of Descartes and the Enlightenment. In this case, these values are embodied in a tidy triangle in which there is no room for depicting the messy contingencies, the pleasant eccentricities, and the intractable concreteness of persons in predicaments. In short, there is in this triangle no trace of those tokens which render so vivid and potent Percy's earlier attack upon the very tradition of which these values are the heart.

This tension, so sharp and clear in "The Delta Factor," informs all of Percy's work. Thus the first essay in *The Message in the Bottle* provides an excellent context in which to get our conceptual bearings. The business of the next two chapters will accordingly be to explore further, in the context of three novels and several other essays, Percy's strengths and weaknesses as a theoretician in both senses discussed in this chapter. At all points the question we must keep before us is this: How and to what extent does the art of the storyteller help us to heal the hurts of the riven self, making it whole once again?

II ♨

Percy as Storyteller

OR, HOW TO AVOID GETTING ZAPPED
BY THE RAVENING PARTICLES

Sometime ago he had discovered that it is impossible to look at a painting simply so: man-looking-at-a-painting, *voila!*—no, it is necessary to play a trick such as watching a man who is watching, standing on his shoulders, so to speak. There are several ways of getting around the ravenous particles.
WALKER PERCY
The Last Gentleman

All sorrows can be borne if you put them into a story or tell a story about them.
ISAK DINESEN
"Three Acre Sorrow"

WALKER PERCY'S second novel, *The Last Gentleman,* begins with this sentence: "One fine day in early summer a young man lay thinking in Central Park."[1] This young man, we soon learn, is one Williston Bibb Barrett—also known as "the engineer"—a Mississippi native and a most amiable if somewhat abstracted individual. We soon learn, too, that he is not entirely well and suffers frequent "spells" during which he is liable to forget his own rather impressive name and wander for weeks at a time amongst the Civil War battlefields of Virginia and other similarly haunted places. Barrett is also possessed of an uncommonly acute "radar," a mixed blessing in that it not only helps him to know what other folk are about (often before they know it themselves) but also makes him especially vulnerable to attack by the "ravening particles," cer-

1. Walker Percy, *The Last Gentleman* (New York, 1966), 3. Subsequent references appear in the text in parentheses; *The Last Gentleman* is abbreviated LG.

tain zinging, noxious particles which clog the air and come between our young man and his tenuous hold on reality. Thus is he reduced to careening about old battlefields paralyzed with anxiety and amnesia. The prognosis is not good.

Much like the Martian in "The Delta Factor," the ravenous particles are an important conceit in *The Last Gentleman*. Appearing like birds of ill omen whenever some especially despairing business is afoot, the particles seem to steal the very substance from both objects and persons, leaving them washed out and, in the case of the latter, prey to vague anxieties and bereft of any sense of sovereignty over their lives. While his peculiar sensitivity enables him to "see" the particles and therefore know why he feels so bad, Barrett is by no means their sole target. On the contrary, everyone suffers their deadening effects, the exact nature of which becomes clear early in the novel when Will visits the Metropolitan Museum of Art. There he finds the air "as thick as mustard gas with ravenous particles which were stealing the substance from painting and viewer alike" (LG, 26). Despite the correct lighting, proper frames, etc., the paintings are "all but impossible to see. . . . The harder one looked the more invisible [they] became" (LG, 27). As for the museum patrons, they are even worse off, as Barrett observes:

> From his vantage point behind the pillar, he noticed that the people who came in were both happy and afflicted. They were afflicted in their happiness. They were serene, but their serenity was a perilous thing to see. In they came, smiling, and out they went, their eyes glazed over. The paintings smoked and shriveled in their frames. (LG, 27)

Suddenly and quite literally out of the blue, help comes in the form of a workman who falls from a skylight far above. Miraculously unhurt, he, Barrett, and a family nearby are covered with finely powdered glass. No less miraculously, the ravening particles are instantly dissipated and both persons and paintings regain substance and become visible again. As he and the family minister to the workman, Barrett chances to look up:

> It was at this moment that the engineer happened to look under his arm and catch sight of the Velázquez. It was glowing like a

jewel! The painter might have just stepped out of his studio and the engineer, passing in the street, had stopped to look through the open door.

The paintings could be seen. (LG, 28)

It would seem, then, that one way to "get around the ravenous particles" is to have a workman fall upon you from a museum skylight. If, however, this cure seems more dangerous than the disease, there is another less perilous therapy implicated in this scene, one that has to do with the role of the storyteller as theorist. On the heels of the passage above, the narrator observes, "He had, of course, got everything turned around. . . . If there were any 'noxious particles' around, they were more likely to be found inside his head than in the sky" (LG, 28–29). In one perfectly obvious sense, we could dismiss the alleged existence of the ravenous particles as merely another symptom of Barrett's illness. While we might be clinically correct to do so, to leave it at that would be to overlook the real significance of this episode both in terms of *The Last Gentleman* per se and of the more catholic concerns of this essay. Quite apart from the question as to whether the noxious particles are "inside his head" or "in the sky," the scene in the museum not only discloses what Percy is about in *The Last Gentleman* but, more important, may be read as a parable of what it means alternately to take up the philosophical essay and the novel or story as an instrument for reflection. As such, this episode comprises a framework from which we may conveniently attend to the larger issue of Percy's effectiveness as a theorist of man in a narrative context.

How are we to interpret this parable? First we must recall two points made earlier. In the Prologue I observed that the Greek word for knowledge, *epistēmē*, whence the English *epistemology*, means literally, "a placing of oneself in the position required for." Knowledge, then, and, by implication, all our feats of knowing require that we dwell in the world in a particular way; hence our way of knowing and our way of being are congruent and cannot be separated. Later, in Chapter I, I argued that truth is dramatic and agonistic; that its apprehension arises in that space of appearance created when one person speaks and another listens and speaks in turn; and that this space of appearance is the dwelling place of reality itself. Now, with these points newly in hand, think again about the scene in the museum. The difficulty facing Will and the others is at once an epistemological and an ontological one. Coming between persons and persons, persons and paintings, the zinging particles have the effect of at best clouding and at worst blotting out altogether that space of appearance without which the reality of individuals and paintings alike evaporates, bereft of its habitation. Thus deprived, each person is profoundly isolated and reduced to a perilous, glassy-eyed "serenity." To echo Arendt, nothing around them possesses that reality guaranteed by the presence of others. Instead, the world and they in it have a dreamlike quality, coming and passing away without substance or reality.

This is the situation which obtains until the workman falls from on high. It is not, however, entirely seamless. His radar going at full power, Will's place in this before-the-fall scene is different from that of his fellows, and that difference provides a clue as to why the great crash is so restorative. Central to the engineer's strategy for besting the noxious particles is that he place himself in a certain position relative to the others in the room—*e.g.*, behind a pillar or, figuratively, on someone's shoulders. This "trick" as he calls it enables him to at least momentarily "get around the ravenous particles." In epistemological terms, we might say that, as a knower, Will stands in relation to the world quite differently from his peers. This is because he has chosen a certain framework in accordance with which his understanding of the world unfolds. Moreover, this framework is felicitous insofar as it empowers him to recognize the serenity of his peers for what it is, empty and perilous. Thus he literally and figuratively "places himself in the position required for" seeing persons and paintings as they actually are.

To borrow a phrase from *The Moviegoer*'s Binx Bolling, Will is definitely "onto something." As Kierkegaard might put it, his is the advantage of the despairing man who knows he is in despair.[2] Our young man's hold upon this advantage is not at all secure, however, and "tricks" notwithstanding, he soon bends to the awful weight of the

2. Cf. Søren Kierkegaard, *Sickness Unto Death*, trans. Walter Lowrie (Princeton, 1968), 177: "The despairing man who is unconscious of being in despair is in comparison with him who is conscious of it, merely a negative step further from the truth and from salvation."

noxious particles. "It was," the narrator tells us, "all he could do to keep from sinking to all fours" (LG, 27). Why is Will unable to sustain his resistance? It is because that epistemological framework which empowers him in one respect constrains him in another; or, more to the point, the indications and standards imposed by that framework are such that they effect a decidedly *in*felicitous change in his being. Specifically, the engineer makes a mistake analogous to that of Martian-novelist-Percy in "The Delta Factor." Barrett's instinct that to make sense of the human world one must look at it from something other than the same old tired perspectives and think about it with something other than the same old tired conceptual tools is quite correct. Throughout the novel this instinct stands him in good stead, but only up to a point. In the pinch, he goes astray in the same way as does Percy-as-Martian. Priding himself on being "scientifically minded," Will confuses an appropriate detachment from old perspectives and old conceptual tools with the inappropriate and godlike detachment of the Cartesian philosopher-observer. Of course, the unassuming engineer would never consciously aspire to such dizzy heights; he has enough trouble just remembering who and where he is. Nevertheless, almost everything about him—his aimless and solitary life; his amnesia; his most prized possession, a powerful, German-made telescope; his peculiarly abstracted "love" for Kitty Vaught; and perhaps most telling, his favorite role, that of an English detective consummately skilled in the art of dispassionate observation—attests to his fundamental ontological state as one who watches and listens and sees but who never commits himself through speech and action to another person.[3]

In short, for all his acuity, friendliness, and basic decency, Will's relation to the human world is unhappily like that ascribed by Percy to Helen Keller—*i.e.*, he is no more than tenuously connected to that world through word and deed. Thus deprived of any space of appear-

3. The role of "eavesdropper" is one which Will often imagines for himself. The following passage is typical: "The engineer . . . read books of great particularity, such as English detective stories, especially the sort which, answering a need of the Anglo-Saxon soul, depict the hero as perfectly disguised or perfectly hidden for days at a time in a burrow of ingenious construction from which he could notice things, observe the farmhouse below. Englishmen like to see without being seen. They are by nature eavesdroppers. The engineer could understand this" (LG, 161–62).

ance in Arendt's sense, his hold on reality is finally no more secure than that of the sundry folk he spies on from behind a pillar or from some imaginary detective's burrow in Somerset. In the idiom of W. H. Auden, "His person has become a fiction; [his] true existence / Is decided by no one and has no importance to love" (*For the Time Being*).

Wherein lies the efficacy, then, of the great crash? The key here is that very thing so conspicuously absent from the scene before the crash, namely, conviviality. Before the workman falls, each person in the room is sunk in himself, "bogged down" as Will puts it. The sudden crash wrests each from his isolation and unites him with the others by virtue of their mutual danger, surprise, and after a moment, relief at having escaped injury. It is this newfound conviviality which dispels the murk of noxious particles. Light and substance are restored to the world and both persons and paintings can suddenly be seen with new clarity.

Notice that as in the context of developing an alternative model of theory based upon storytelling, we find once again the concepts "clarity" and "conviviality" in close, friendly, and therefore unconventional proximity to one another. In this second appearance of the odd couple lies the heart of our parable. First, it is significant that the physical appearance of Barrett and the others is momentarily altered by a shower of fine glass:

> For there he was, the worker, laid out and powdered head to toe like a baker. Some seconds passed before the engineer realized that it was glass that turned him white, glass powdered to sugar. It covered the family too. They stood for an age gazing at each other, turned into pillars of salt; then, when they saw that no one was hurt, they fell into one another's arms, weeping and laughing. (LG, 28)

This transformation, which we might expect to be a source of additional confusion, even fear, has in fact a strangely liberating effect, a paradox which must not pass unnoticed. To use St. Paul's image, it is as if before they saw through a glass darkly but now they see face to face (I Corinthians 13:12). What does it mean in this context "to see face to face"? It does not mean here any more than in Corinthians to see with perfect lucidity and in the instant all the world arrayed before one. Moreover, it is conspicuously not the case that the clarity issues from the deliberate marshaling of clear and distinct ideas. On the contrary, that clarity is implicated or *folded into* the incident itself. Further, the simple fact that the stuff of the incident is an indecorous mix of the accidental, the destructive, and the life-threatening lends additional credence to the thesis that the clarity which obtains after the crash does not fit the Cartesian model. Instead, "to see face to face" is to know and value the concreteness and particularity of both self and other; it is to feel their fragility in the neighborhood of injury and death and to rejoice nonetheless. Most important, this new knowledge cannot be abstracted from the situation in which Barrett and the others find themselves. It is not a moveable feast. Rather, logically of a piece with the nature of truth itself, this knowledge is dramatic and agonistic and not to be had apart from a convivial setting.

In this connection, it is of no small significance that, for Will at least, the salubrious effect of this incident does not last. The next morning, solitary once again, he buys the telescope, convinced that the lenses "penetrated to the heart of things"[4] (LG, 29). Like Tom More of *Love in the Ruins*, with his Quantitative Qualitative Ontological Lapsometer, Will Barrett unwittingly and to his cost chooses his weapon from the arsenal of the enemy. In a way perfectly analogous to Martian-essayist-Percy's reliance upon the tokens of behaviorism in "The Delta Factor," the telescope just as surely blinds Will to the appropriate implications of his sense that he and his fellows are in deep trouble. Instead of true conviviality, it provides an artificial closeness in which people, no less than individual bricks in a far building, are reduced to the status of objects to be observed in a noncommittal way. Hence, as do Helen Keller, the liquid water, and the word *water* in Percy's "The Delta Factor" triangle, so do persons, bricks, and anything else within the telescope's range enjoy an equal ontological footing when viewed through the mechanical eye. Rather than "recovering things" as Will hopes, his fine instrument only pushes them farther away, making him more vulnerable than ever to attack by the ravening particles.

Thus is the episode in the art museum divided neatly in two by the workman's fall from the skylight. The reason why this is worth re-

4. Walker Percy, *The Moviegoer* (New York, 1960), 120. Subsequent references appear in the text in parentheses; *The Moviegoer* is abbreviated MG.

marking at length should be clear when we consider the implications of the similarities between Will Barrett in this episode and Percy-as-Martian in "The Delta Factor." As we have seen, two importantly different models of theory and clarity are at work for Percy in the opening essay of *The Message in the Bottle*. Further, his use of the Cartesian model is decidedly infelicitous, while his use of a narrative model has much happier results. The case can now be made that the scene in the Metropolitan recapitulates in narrative terms the strengths and weaknesses, the sundry pretensions and intentions of Percy's argument in that essay—*i.e.*, Will Barrett's ups and downs, his insight pitted against his penchant for detachment are the very embodiment of Percy's own profound intellectual ambivalence and confusion in "The Delta Factor."

How so? The onto-epistemic situation which obtains before the crash is logically of a piece with that which obtains when Percy takes up the conceptual tools of Cartesianism and launches a frontal assault on the regnant philosophical tradition of the West. Like Will, the harder he looks, the less he sees. To put it differently, the epistemology and ontology folded into this phenomenon is analogous to that implied in the phenomenon of writing a philosophical essay the aim of which is to dismantle the Cartesian picture of the self but in which the author relies upon the philosophical dispositions which uphold that picture. Just as the ravenous particles clog the air in the museum, cutting Will and the others off from one another, so do the analogies, metaphors, images, and rhetorical strategies that comprise the Cartesian framework come between Percy-as-essayist and his roots in the human world of actors and speakers.

In contrast, the onto-epistemic situation which obtains after the crash is logically homogeneous with that which obtains for Percy when he puts his critique of modern culture into a story; or, in the case of "The Delta Factor," in the context of "little dramas" and linguistic tokens whose bent is toward the concrete, the active, and the incarnate. The way of knowing and being implied in the phenomenon of seeing persons and paintings clearly because one has been forcefully remanded to the concrete world in which death may come suddenly and in which the lived mind-body and the company of one's fellows are thereby made precious is analogous to that implied in the phenomenon of storytelling. The workman's fall renders the activity of *mere spectation* conspicuously inappropriate to the situation at hand; so too does the storyteller's language game render the regnant model of reflection inappropriate as a tool with which to think about the nature of man in the postmodern age. It provides instead an instrument much better suited to the task of thinking about a creature in which Word and Flesh struggle to become one.

I have suggested that the tension so evident in "The Delta Factor" between two radically different ways of thinking about man informs all of Percy's work. Here in this brief episode from *The Last Gentleman* we find that tension equally sharp. The important difference and the important point is that as the author of *The Last Gentleman* Percy is no less aware of Will Barrett's weaknesses and the inadequacy of his orientation to the world than he is of his singular gifts. By placing this particular character in a particular situation, he clearly and concretely illustrates the pernicious effects of even the most tacit acquiescence to the dicta of Cartesianism vis-à-vis the self. As the author of "The Delta Factor," however, he seems unaware of this proclivity in himself. More precisely, he is unaware of it when as the author of the second major part of "The Delta Factor" he abandons the pleasantly "unedifying" language game of the storyteller in favor of the decidedly edifying one of the closet behaviorist.

Thus this dense episode from Percy's second novel seems to bear out the thesis that Percy thinks most clearly when he uses the novel rather than the philosophical essay as his instrument for reflection. The implications of this scene are borne out in his first and third novels and in two essays from *The Message in the Bottle* as well. There we shall find that so long as he employs the tokens and follows the pretensions of the storyteller's language game, Percy is consistently successful at "getting around the ravenous particles"—*i.e.*, at sustaining an attack upon the philosophic tradition of the West that is unerring in its accuracy and devastating in its potency.

EARLIER, I observed that Will Barrett and Binx Bolling, protagonist of *The Moviegoer*, have at least one thing in common: they are both "onto something." What Binx is onto is "the search," and like Will's clairvoyance in the matter of ravenous particles, his clear sense of both the possibility and the necessity of embarking upon the search is our best clue as to how things stand with him. Just what the search is and how it is apposite to his predicament is the heart of the novel, and there we shall focus our attention. Specifically, I want to suggest that Binx's predicament is analogous to that of Will Barrett in the museum before the crash; his situation too bears the unmistakable mark of our culture's tacit and wholesale adherence to the Cartesian picture of the self. Further, like the workman's fall, the way out of that predicament implicated in "the search" brings together certain concepts judged logically heterogeneous according to the Cartesian framework. Like that of Barrett, Binx's predicament may thus be shown to reflect Percy's firm grasp of the conceptual issues at stake in a narrative critique of Cartesianism.

What exactly is Binx's predicament? There is nothing which immediately suggests itself as a source of difficulty. He is young, attractive, and intelligent. He has plenty of money and enjoys making it as a stockbroker. Unlike Will Barrett, he does not suffer from amnesia or any other peculiar ailments. He is fond of women and they of him. It is true that his father was afflicted with melancholy and died a rather too romantic death, drowned in the sea off Crete, a copy of *A Shropshire Lad* in his pocket. Binx finds this recollection troubling at times but is more often simply puzzled and bemused by his sense that it is somehow a clue in his search; exactly how and why is unclear.

In what way, then, might we say that Binx is a man in a predicament? First, like Barrett he knows that, the pleasantries of life notwithstanding, all is not well. More than once he refers to the spoiler as "the malaise": "What is the malaise? you ask. The malaise is the pain of loss. The world is lost to you, the world and the people in it, and there remains only you and the world and you no more able to be in the world than Banquo's ghost."[4] Consider carefully what Binx is saying here. The "ghost at a feast" image is one which we have seen Percy use in "The Delta Factor" to describe the plight of modern man exiled from the world, ironically, by the very science which has transformed that world for his benefit and comfort. As one who feels that exile keenly, Binx speaks right to the heart of the dilemma. Indeed, his definition of the malaise might equally be described as a concise statement of what it is like to live as though the Cartesian picture of the self up-held by modern science were exhaustively true; as though the "I" were synonymous with a discarnate mind reluctantly inhabiting an insensate body and loosed upon a world of equally insensate and hostile objects.

Binx's remark is particularly arresting not merely because it is succinct; its real potency lies in its *situatedness*. When he speaks of the loss of the world, his fellows, and consequently of himself, Binx does not do so as one who makes an abstract philosophical proposition which might be uttered by Anyone, Anyplace. Instead, he speaks as one man to another ("What is the malaise? *you ask*.") and as one who feels the pain of this loss on ordinary Wednesday mornings in old New Orleans. To put it simply, the sense of loss that haunts Binx cannot be abstracted from a particular person who finds himself in a particular predicament; it *cannot be* apart from Binx's story. So obvious that its significance might be overlooked, this fact is most important. By presenting us not with sweeping generalizations about modern culture or the nature of modern man but rather with one John Bickerson Bolling, a certain man who finds himself in a certain situation, Percy effectively stretches our minds and imaginations away from that habit of thought governed by the spirit of abstraction. As in the first pages of "The Delta Factor," he invites us instead to attend both *from* and *to* the particulars of persons in predicaments, our reflections pretended by the concrete tokens of the storyteller's language game.

Binx's economical response to the question "What is the malaise?" is neither the first nor the last time the long shadow of Descartes falls across his story. The loss of world, self, and other implicit in Cartesian thought makes itself felt at almost every turn. Three passages are especially telling in this regard. Two involve Binx alone while the third includes his cousin, Kate Cutrer, and each gives evidence of Percy's firm control over his conceptual territory.

Very early in the novel, Binx tells us something about his life—his family, his brokerage business, his domestic arrangements in the suburb of Gentilly, and the special pleasure he takes in going to movies. The only thing remarkable in all this is that Binx's life seems as unremarkable as the suburb in which he lives. Indeed, he sets great store by being so unexceptional; it is a trait he cultivates assiduously. Of particular interest in the present context is what by Binx's own estimation gives this quiet life shape and coherence:

> Life in Gentilly is very peaceful. . . . I am a model tenant and a model citizen and take pleasure in doing all that is expected of me. My wallet is full of identity cards, library cards, credit cards. . . . It is a pleasure to carry out the duties of a citizen and to receive in return a receipt or a neat styrene card with one's name on it certifying, so to speak, one's right to exist. (MG, 6–7)

No less pointedly than do the images in "The Delta Factor" of sundry folk feeling good in bad environments and vice versa, Binx's self-portrait attests to the poverty of a picture of the self which divorces mind from body and denies both any purchase or status in the human world of speech and action. How so? In Binx's case the bankruptcy of such a picture is embodied quite vividly in his belief that his identity is contingent upon that most impersonal and featureless of modern inventions, the plastic credit card. Only by keeping a firm grip on his wallet full of cards and by "doing all that is expected of [him]," can Binx reassure himself that he does indeed exist. Thus for the present at least, when called upon to give an account of himself *as a self*, Binx does not do so in terms of speech and action. The tokens which do come to hand are abstracted from any plexus of words, deeds, and human relationships and are informed instead by one of the principle theses of Cartesian thought, namely, that mathematics is the measure of all things. The move from this notion to that which posits one's "right to exist" in numbers on a card (numbers which might equally be assigned to Anyone, Anyplace, Anytime) is neither far nor difficult.

Binx has been reduced to this unhappy state precisely because the potent though unobtrusive legacy of the Enlightenment is such that he is constrained to think of the self in just these terms at the exclusion of all others; most particularly, at the exclusion of any model or conceptual framework which acknowledges the fact of our embodiment. Later, recalling his reading habits before getting onto the search, Binx realizes the price of this exclusion:

Until recent years, I read only "fundamental" books, that is, key books on key subjects. . . . During those years, I stood outside the universe and sought to understand it. I lived in my room as an Anyone living Anywhere and read fundamental books and only for diversion took walks around the neighborhood and saw an occasional movie. Certainly it did not matter to me where I was when I read such a book as *The Expanding Universe*. . . . The only difficulty was that though the universe had been disposed of, I myself was left over. There I lay in my hotel room with my search over yet still obliged to draw one breath and then the next. (MG, 69–70)[5]

The echo here of the charge Kierkegaard leveled against Hegel, namely, that he had built a large and beautiful structure in which to house everything in the universe save himself, who must live outside in a miserable hut, is unmistakable.[6] It would not be overstating the case to say that Binx no less than Søren Kierkegaard has stumbled upon the best-kept secret of modern philosophy: If a man tries to live according to the precepts of that philosophy, he will inevitably find himself as homeless as Ishmael and a castaway twice over—first, cast out of Eden and condemned to know the pain of death and of God's silence; and then cast out of himself so that the personal pronoun "I" is emptied out, bereft of any habitation in the city of man. Thus is the world outside the garden equally lost to him. This is precisely the dilemma Binx embodies in the guise of "Anyone living Anywhere" with a pocketful of credit cards and reading "fundamental" books. The one question his books cannot answer is that which Percy, like Kierkegaard, keeps always in hand: What is it to be a man and to live and die?

The toll so quietly and relentlessly taken upon the human spirit by the struggle to live up to the demands of being Anyone, Anyplace is

5. The search he refers to here is his "vertical search" as distinct from the later "horizontal search." It is the latter which Binx has in mind when he feels he is "onto something."

6. See Søren Kierkegaard, *The Journals of Søren Kierkegaard: A Selection*, ed. and trans. Alexander Dru (London, 1938), Paragraph #583, p. 156: "In relation to their systems most systematisers are like a man who builds an enormous castle and lives in a shack close by; they do not live in their own enormous systematic buildings. But spiritually that is a decisive objection. Spiritually speaking, a man's thought must be the building in which he lives—otherwise everything is topsy-turvy."

almost always before us in *The Moviegoer*. Perhaps nowhere in the novel is that toll so distressingly clear as near the end when Binx and Kate make love on the train going to Chicago. The relationship between these two is an important part of the novel and plays an important role in the progress of Binx's search. Being in a somewhat precarious mental state, Kate is especially vulnerable to the malaise. Always either falling behind herself or leaping ahead of herself, as Binx puts it, she never quite comes to rest, never quite coincides with herself. Consequently, she is rather like Tom More of *Love in the Ruins* and subject to night exaltations and morning terrors. For all of that, however, she is a most thoughtful and intelligent young woman who knows she is in a predicament. In this, she and Binx have much in common and so are drawn together.

At the novel's end, Kate and Binx are married. This commitment is possible, however, only after they have tasted together the bitter despair of knowing that "flesh poor flesh" cannot *of itself* rescue one from the numbing effects of the malaise:

> Flesh poor flesh failed us. The burden was too great and flesh poor flesh, neither hallowed by sacrament nor despised by spirit (for despising is not the worst fate to overtake the flesh), but until this moment seen through and cancelled, rendered null by the cold and fishy eye of the malaise—flesh poor flesh now at this moment summoned all at once to be all and everything, end all and be all, the last and only hope—quails and fails. The truth is that I was frightened half to death by her bold (not really bold, not whorish bold but *theorish* bold) carrying on. . . . Kate too was scared. We shook like leaves. (MG, 200. Emphasis mine.)

The burden under which Binx and Kate labor does not issue from the absence of love and care. Their difficulty lies in being without a human habitation for that love and care. The discovery they make is that the flesh has been so thoroughly and systematically nullified by the logical dominance of mind in modern culture that the living body has become in effect exactly as Descartes said—not significantly different from the flesh of a corpse. It is a nothing, a zero, "mere flesh." As such, it is equally unfit as a vessel for love or hate but is simply empty. Consequently, like those scientists in *Love in the Ruins* who are utterly abstracted from the ordinary world and seek to reenter it by engaging in the most bestial behavior, so do Binx and Kate demand too much of "flesh poor flesh" and likewise fail.

As painful as it is, however, their failure is neither final nor complete because they have the advantage of knowing themselves to be in a predicament. The clue to the resolution of that predicament evident in their eventual marriage lies in the nature of the search. And what is that exactly? Binx has this to say:

> The search is what anyone would undertake if he were not sunk in the everydayness of his own life. This morning, for example, I felt as if I had come to myself on a strange island. And what does such a castaway do? Why, he pokes around the neighborhood and doesn't miss a trick.
>
> To become aware of the possibility of the search is to be onto something. Not to be onto something is to be in despair. (MG, 13)

The notion of "coming to oneself" and the image of the castaway turn up often in Percy's writing and do important work in each instance. Usually the former occurs as a result of some disaster which shakes one loose from the grip of "everydayness." Binx, we learn, came to himself lying on the ground under a chindolea bush in Korea in 1951, seriously wounded in the shoulder. What should have been a very bad time for him was, in typical Percian inside-out fashion, a very good one. Why? It was good because all that had been lost to him in the malaise was momentarily recovered, and for a brief time everything was imbued with an astonishing substance and reality. Like the paintings in the Metropolitan after the crash, things could be seen. Binx goes on to say, "As I watched, there awoke in me an immense curiosity. I was onto something. I vowed that if I ever got out of this fix, I would pursue the search" (MG, 11). Binx can never say precisely what is the object of his search and is always on the lookout for clues—*e.g.*, his father, the Jews, movies. Moreover, for long stretches he loses entirely his sense of being "onto something" but sooner or later it returns to him, always unexpected and usually prompted by his being suddenly struck with the splendid presence and concreteness of some person or object or scene.

The other important notion here is implicit in the image of the castaway. The particular sort of castaway Binx has in mind here is not the one who "comes to himself in a strange place . . . and settles down with a vengeance. In two weeks time, he is so sunk in everydayness that he might just as well be dead" (MG, 13). Rather Binx's castaway is a seeker who, to borrow an image from "The Message in the Bottle," never forgets he is not at home and awaits the newsbearer who can tell him who he is and where home is. An important part of being onto something and so avoiding the worst sort of despair is just this awareness. It is to know that one's self is not equivalent to the sum of the particulars of one's everyday life.

This image of the castaway, together with the notion of coming to oneself, suggests that at stake in the search is nothing less than the acknowledgment and acceptance of that tension between immanence and transcendence which makes us what we humanly are as selves. When Binx "comes to himself" under the chindolea bush, the world that had been lost to him, including his own body, is given back in all its concreteness, in all its unyielding immanence. At the same moment, however, he is filled with, as he says, "an immense curiosity" and becomes henceforth "a seeker." The world recovered, Binx knows himself to be very much in the world and rejoices in its and his concrete reality. Yet he also knows himself not to be exhaustively defined by that world; he is a castaway the secret of whose identity is held by one across the sea.

Whereas flesh, poor flesh must fail Kate and Binx when they demand that it be the repository *simpliciter* of their respective selves, to acknowledge that same flesh as the necessary ground of but not equivalent to "an Otherness that can say 'I'" [7] is to be onto something very precious indeed. Thus Binx's search promises to be a fine antidote to the malaise. But does what we learn in the epilogue seem to bear out this hope? Given his marriage to Kate, his plans to go to medical school, etc., we might think that Binx gives up the search and succumbs to that very everydayness he so wishes to avoid. Percy himself suggests another interpretation, however, when he says that, in

7. W. H. Auden, *For the Time Being*, 176. From a three-line speech of the wise men in the section titled "At the Manger," the passage in full is quite appropriate to the present context: "The singular is not love's enemy; / Love's possibilities of realization / Require an Otherness that can say *I*."

Kierkegaardian terms, Binx "jumps from the aesthetic mode clear across the ethical to the religious. He has no ethical sphere at all."[8] This remark seems quite appropriate to Binx's situation when we remember that in Kierkegaard's account of the Abraham and Isaac story Abraham returns from Mount Moriah and says nothing to Sarah of his experience. Instead, he goes quietly about his business looking and speaking like the most ordinary tax collector. The knight of faith is always so disguised: "Those . . . who carry the jewel of faith are likely to be delusive because their outward appearance bears a striking resemblance to that which both the infinite resignation and faith profoundly despise . . . to Philistinism."[9] In this improbable knight, the immanent and the transcendent come together with a serenity that is not empty and perilous like that of Will Barrett's fellow museum goers. Rather, his is a serenity born of the redemption of the mundane world achieved, paradoxically, by his first giving it up and then believing past all reckoning that he will be given it back again. Simply put, the knight of faith rejoices in the beauty of his island even as he discovers himself to be a castaway who can never be fully at home on that island.

One more point needs to be made about Kierkegaard's knight of faith, and it is most important. In Kierkegaard's view, that which makes Abraham the knight of faith is not contemplation but action. Further, the test to which God puts him is no test apart from the value placed upon the temporal and mundane love of father for son and the promise of descendants "countless as the dust of the earth" (Genesis 13:16). Faith, then, is not a moveable feast, for it has no meaning, no habitation apart from the terrible predicament of one man. It is rather profoundly *situated* in the world, in the lived mind-body. There and only there may the transcendent, nonspecifiable "I" appear. Thus does Kierkegaard redeem the self from both the limits of "flesh poor flesh" and the homelessness of disembodied mind.

Now in the case of Binx, we do not, of course, have such a dramatic test of faith as God's command to Abraham that he sacrifice Isaac.

8. John Carr, "An Interview with Walker Percy," *Georgia Review*, XXV (Fall, 1971), 327.
9. Søren Kierkegaard, *Fear and Trembling*, trans. Walter Lowrie (Princeton, 1941), 49.

Even so, the Binx of the novel's close has undergone some subtle and important changes which indicate that he has made the movement of faith. For instance, his secretary-chasing days over, his and Kate's "frail enterprise in love" has matured into marriage.[10] Aunt Emily has admitted that he is "not one of her heroes but a very ordinary fellow"; consequently, they get along much better than before. When his fifteen-year-old half brother dies of a massive infection, Binx answers truthfully when asked by the other children if Lonnie is going to die. He also answers their other and perhaps more difficult questions with compassion and without the slightest hesitation:

> "Binx . . . when our Lord raises us up on the last day, will Lonnie still be in a wheelchair or will he be like us?"
> "He'll be like you."
> "You mean he'll be able to ski?" The children cock their heads and listen like old men.
> "Yes." (MG, 240)

Perhaps most telling, he has only this to say about his search:

> As for my search, I have not the inclination to say much on the subject. For one thing, I have not the authority as the great Danish philosopher declared, to speak of such matters in any way other than the edifying. For another thing, it is not open to me even to be edifying, since the time is later than his, much too late to edify or do much of anything except plant a foot in the right place as the opportunity presents itself—if indeed asskicking is properly distinguished from edification. (MG, 327)

Typical of the knight of faith, Binx declines to assume the responsibility of one who speaks with authority. That position properly belongs to the apostle or the newsbearer. Instead, he is content to go quietly along his way merely engaging now and then in some helpful asskicking.[11]

10. Brainard Cheney, "To Restore a Fragmented Image," *Sewanee Review*, LXIX (Autumn, 1961), 700.

11. Percy makes another interesting remark when he says Binx is like Alyosha in *The Brothers Karamozov*, in that he tells the truth about Lonnie while Kate wishes to avoid the fact of his imminent death. Such quiet truthfulness is another sign of the knight of faith. See Carr, "An Interview with Walker Percy," 328.

In a word, all that was restless and at times a little manic in Binx has disappeared, to be replaced by a sense of quiet assurance, the assurance of a man at home with the world and with himself. This quiet is not, however, that of dumb passivity. Rather, it is that of a man who stands ready to hear the newsbearer whenever and wherever he appears; of one no longer torn between his island home and his home across the sea but who waits and watches patiently, confident that the news will come one day. Moreover, the faith signified by this posture is not one which permits Binx to follow the example of St. Anthony and withdraw to the desert to await the Lord's coming. Rather, he is called to work in the vineyard, loving, nurturing, and supporting Kate, Aunt Emily, his half brothers and sisters. As he thinks to himself when Kate asks what he plans to do:

> There is only one thing I can do: listen to people, see how they stick themselves into the world, hand them along a ways on their dark journey and be handed along. And for good and selfish reasons. It only remains to decide whether this vocation is best pursued in a service station or—(MG, 233)

As it happens, Binx chooses medical school over the attractive alternative of running a small service station, but the important point is that what he clearly perceives to be his vocation carries him out into the world to "hand people along" and be handed along in turn. It is this— not reading fundamental books, not living as Anyone, Anyplace, not endlessly going to movies—but this care and conviviality for and with the living creature, mortal, guilty, beautiful, which defeats the malaise. Perhaps too this is what it is to be a man and to live and die.

As in *The Last Gentleman*, Percy's modus operandi in *The Moviegoer* is to present us with a person in a predicament. Also as in *The Last Gentleman*, that predicament is closely tied to the influence upon our culture of a certain picture of the self implicit in the dominant philosophic tradition of the West. Thus Percy chooses for himself as author and for us as readers a certain framework and certain conceptual tools with which to consider the efficacy of that picture. The ensuing critique is both conceptually clear and polemically on target, demonstrating once again the acuity of his insight into the whys and wherefores of man's terrible unhappiness in the twentieth century. Too it lends further support to my thesis that as an instrument for reflection, storytelling is superior to abstract philosophical argument when it comes to thinking about and perhaps even alleviating that unhappinesss. *Love in the Ruins* will provide even more support for both these points.

THE FINE WIT and sense of irony evident in both *The Moviegoer* and *The Last Gentleman* together with the singular liberties available to the satirist make *Love in the Ruins* a wickedly funny and polemically devastating novel. In the story of Thomas More, M.D., widower, psychiatrist, alcoholic, and self-proclaimed bad Catholic (but a believer nonetheless), Percy takes deadly aim at the more conspicuous insanities of "the Christ-forgetting, Christ-haunted death-dealing Western world." [12] Almost no one escapes his satiric reach: liberals, conservatives, blacks, whites, Roman Catholics, Protestants—just to name a few—are equally chastised for their complicity in the imminent demise of Western culture.

At the heart of that demise is what Tom More is pleased to call "More's syndrome, or: chronic angelism-bestialism that rives soul from body and sets it orbiting the great world as the spirit of abstraction whence it takes the form of beasts, swans and bulls, werewolves, bloodsuckers, Mr. Hydes, or just poor lonesome ghost locked in its own machinery" (LR, 383). Thanks to Percy's judicious use of the satirist's license for hyperbole, it is at once amusingly and painfully clear that this "chronic-angelism-bestialism" riddles the novel's private and public worlds and that it sets every man equally against his neighbor and himself, diagnostician More no less than the others. It is in this world that Thomas More, M.D., distant kinsman of Sir Thomas More ("Why can't I follow More's example, love myself less, God and my fellow man more, and leave whiskey and women alone?") bravely and not too humbly ("I am . . . nevertheless a genius . . . who sees into the hidden causes of things and erects simple hypotheses to account for the glut of everyday events.") sets out to "weld the broken self whole" (LR, 23, 11, 36). The tool with which he hopes to accomplish this feat

12. Walker Percy, *Love in the Ruins* (New York, 1971), 3. Subsequent references appear in the text in parentheses; *Love in the Ruins* is abbreviated LR.

is an unprepossessing little gadget dubbed "More's Quantitative Qualitative Ontological Lapsometer." "With it," he claims, "any doctor can probe the very secrets of the soul, diagnose the maladies that poison the wellsprings of man's hope. It could save the world or destroy it" (LR, 7).

Tom More and his invention are the center of the novel. What is of particular interest in the present context is the discrepancy between his skills as a diagnostician and his skill at effecting a cure. This discrepancy is not merely a matter of, having once made a diagnosis, being uncertain as to the correct prescription. Rather, it reflects a profound confusion analogous to that evident in Percy himself in "The Delta Factor." Having made an astute diagnosis of certain peculiarly modern maladies afflicting body and spirit alike, More is then seduced by modern science, in the rather scruffy guise of one Art Immelman, into believing that if we just had the right machine and could tinker with the right brain cells, all could be made well. As we have seen in "The Delta Factor," this is rather like setting the fox to guard the henhouse, and More's enterprise meets with about as much success. The important point, however, is that, as we have seen in the predicament of Will Barrett and Binx Bolling, Percy is well aware of More's weakness and confusion and is, by implication, fully in control of his material.

The extent to which this is the case is particularly clear in the doctor's dealings with Immelman. Looking like "the sort of fellow who used to service condom vendors in the old Auto Age," Art plays an appropriately deadbeat Mephistopheles to More's alcoholic Faust. Percy once remarked, "The great difference between Dr. More and the other heroes is that Dr. More has no philosophical problems. He knows what he believes."[13] He might have added that More also knows what he likes and in what order: "I believe in God and the whole business but I love women best, music and science next, whiskey next, God fourth, and my fellow man hardly at all. Generally I do as I please" (LR, 6). It is to this hierarchy that Art appeals when he offers More the one thing he cannot resist, the power to know and love

13. Zoltan, Abadi-Nagy, "A Talk with Walker Percy," *Southern Literary Journal*, VI (Fall, 1973), 6.

and to win at both. Significantly, "to know" means here to know abstractly; "to love" means to love not a particular woman but all women. As Art puts it:

> You stimulate the scientist-lover . . . so that in the same moment one becomes victorious in science one also becomes victorious in love. And all for the good of mankind! Science to help all men and a happy joyous love to help all women. . . . This love has its counterpart in scientific knowledge: it is neutral morally, abstractive and godlike . . . in the sense of being like a god in one's freedom and omniscience. (LR, 213–14)

The prospect of becoming Faust and Don Juan all at once is too much for More to resist. But how is the shaky doctor to be so transformed, and what is the price? We all know the devil gives away nothing for free.

The answer lies in More's invention. An experienced encephalographer, he has a hunch that with a wireless gadget similar to an encephalograph he might be able to measure electrical activity in specific areas of the brain. With a little help from a colleague, he puts just such a machine together. The problem remaining is this: "Given such a machine, given such readings, could the readings then be correlated with the manifold woes of the Western world, its terrors and rages and murderous impulses? And if so, could the latter be treated by treating the former?" (LR, 28–29). More believes the answer is yes if only the right "dosage" could be found.

Eventually Tom succeeds in correlating certain patterns of electrical activity in the brain with various manifestations of chronic angelism-bestialism. Until Art comes along, however, his lapsometer is useful only as a diagnostic tool and not as a therapeutic one. The curious Mr. Immelman, who speaks the worst sort of bureaucratic jargon and always appears and disappears under the most peculiar circumstances, has the answer: an attachment which will enable More to alter these electrical patterns and effect at least a temporary cure for, say, night exaltation, morning terror, conservative fits, radical seizures, and abstracted lust, not to mention large-bowel complaints. In short, he offers More the alleged means by which to cure the very soul of Western man, healing the rift between mind and body by which he was cast out of himself. As if this prospect were not seductive enough, More is also assured, Art tells him, of winning a Nobel Prize. Since he is as vain as he is well-meaning, this last helps him to overcome his vague distrust of Immelman. In return, all he has to do is hand over to Art all his lapsometers plus patent rights.

What is the issue here? The key is "*alleged* means of cure." In the same interview in which Percy commented on More's lack of philosophical problems, he also said this: "The big mistake was in him, that he could believe he could treat a spiritual disease with a scientific device however sophisticated." [14] What More proposes to do with his lapsometer is to fight fire with fire using the conceptual tools of science to compensate for the inadequacies of science. What Percy proposes to do in his "The Delta Factor" triangle is, remember, logically analogous—merely to "improve" upon an old therapy, an old way of thinking about the human creature rather than to develop a radically new therapy and so avoid the conceptual traps so well hidden in the old. The important point is that once again we find that Percy-as-storyteller, in contrast to Percy-as-essayist, is onto the fallacy of this approach.

The evidence that this is so is not confined to a single remark in a single interview. The most substantial proof is in the novel itself. Not only does More's invention exacerbate rather than cure the symptoms of "More's syndrome" and with disastrous results; there is in addition one character who intimates the radical therapy which is the appropriate antidote to chronic angelism-bestialism and which More fails to effect with his invention. The character is Father Smith, priest to the small remnant of a once large Roman Catholic congregation.

Father Smith appears at several important points in the novel. Like More and unlike any other character, he knows that times are very bad and that man is in deep trouble. He does not, however, talk about "chronic angelism-bestialism"; rather he says, "The channels are jammed and the word is not getting through. . . . The news [is] being jammed . . . principalities and powers have won and we've lost . . . death is winning, life is losing" (LR, 185). Obviously, Father Smith is feeling rather low and his response to this dismal situation is signifi-

14. *Ibid.*, 17.

cantly different from More's. Central to the priest's assessment of his and his fellows' predicament is "news"—not brain waves, not heavy sodium and chloride ions, but "news." As we have seen in "The Delta Factor" and shall see again in "The Message in the Bottle," the notion of news is at the heart of what Percy takes to be a coherent theory of man. Moreover, it is "the clue and sign" of man's salvation. That it should turn up here in just this context is most important. Implicit in the priest's suggestion is a conceptual framework which is logically at odds with the scientific and tacitly Cartesian one of More. It is a measure of the latter's obtuseness on this point that, knowing Smith operates a ham radio, Tom dismisses his remark as merely a lapse into ham radio jargon. For his part, the priest does not straighten him out by making his framework explicit. Instead, he simply goes on about his business, hearing confessions, saying the Mass, baptizing the newborn, and burying the dead.

By thus linking news or the lack of it with the unhappy state of affairs he sees around him, the otherwise unremarkable Father Smith makes an important conceptual move which More, constrained as he is by the conceptual framework of science, cannot make. In effect, the priest quietly introduces into the chaos of More's world the possibility of welding the broken self whole by means of an instrument which cannot be manufactured, as can the lapsometer, in an Osaka computer plant. Father Smith's instrument is not a moveable feast. Rather, it is folded into his own speech and action and into the news of which he is the bearer. Further, if the word gets through at all, it will be only to one who knows himself to be in a certain predicament and so stands in the way of hearing news.

Soon after this scene, Father Smith disappears, to reappear only in the epilogue, set at Christmas Eve five years after the main action of the novel. In the interim, society has been burned inside out with the "Bantus" now occupying the top of the economic and social ladder and the white folks the bottom. Not much has really changed, however. The Bantus now suffer night exaltations and morning terrors just like the white man. The local scientists are more abstracted from themselves than ever. The broken self is, in a word, still broken. But two things have changed. First Art Immelman is gone, dispatched by a desperate prayer offered up by Tom More to his kinsman: "Sir Thomas

More, kinsman, saint, best, dearest, merriest of Englishmen, pray for us and drive this son of a bitch hence" (LR, 376). Second, the latter-day More has given up both Early Times and vodka-Tang-duck-egg break-fasts, married Ellen, his rather tart Presbyterian nurse, fathered two children, and makes a very modest living as a physician. He does con-tinue to tinker with his invention and has not quite given up hope that one day he will be able to cure as well as diagnose chronic angelism-bestialism.

An economical way to describe this change in More is to say that he now stands in the way of hearing news. This is not to claim that he has resolved all his difficulties. On the contrary, he frequently yearns for a drink and admits that mornings are "still not the best of times." Even so, More no longer aspires to be either Faust or Don Juan but has settled into a middle place inhabited by neither angels nor beasts:

> Strange: I am older, yet there seems to be more time, time for watching and thinking and working. I am a poor man but a kingly one. If you want and wait and work, you can have. . . . What I want is no longer the Nobel, screw prizes, but just to figure out what I've hit upon. Someday, a man will walk into my office as ghost or beast or ghost-beast and walk out as a man, which is to say sovereign wanderer, lordly exile, worker, and waiter, and watcher. (LR, 384)

In short, More lives in the world in a way quite different from before. Even his lingering aspiration to do that which he probably cannot do reflects this change from Faust/Don Juan to wayfarer/castaway. To go from the lust to know and love abstractly to the relatively modest busi-ness of figuring out what one has "hit upon" and using that discovery to heal is to make an important change indeed. It is one which anchors More and his invention in the mundane and concrete world of actors and speakers.

Pride is tenacious, however, and More is far from being rid of it. When after a hiatus of eleven years he goes to confession on Christmas Eve, he is angry and disappointed when Father Smith seems unim-pressed, even bored, with his catalog of sins and, more important, with the fact that he is not particularly sorry to have committed them. What Smith realizes and More does not is that such sins as Tom's are but a distraction from the more serious ills of the human spirit, which are also more banal. He tells More:

> Meanwhile, forgive me but there are other things we must think about: like doing our jobs, you being a better doctor, I being a better priest, showing a bit of ordinary kindness to people, particularly in our own families—unkindness to those close to us is a pitiful thing—doing what we can for our poor unhappy country—things which, please forgive me, sometimes seem more important than dwelling on a few middle-aged day-dreams.

More finally understands:

> "You're right, I'm sorry," I say instantly, scalded.
> "You're sorry for your sins?"
> "Yes. Ashamed rather."
> "That will do . . . go in peace." (LR, 399)

More does go in peace, humbled when reminded by Father Smith of Jesus' teaching that the first two commandments are greater than all the rest.

Love in the Ruins ends on this note of profound reconciliation. Like Binx Bolling, Tom More has learned to watch and wait and listen even as he rejoices in his wife, his children, and other earthly delights. In his story and most especially in the spectacular failure of More's Quantitative Qualitative Ontological Lapsometer, Percy again exposes the pernicious influence upon our culture and ourselves of the great Cartesian divide. The clarity and potency of his critique further attest to the great heuristic power of the conceptual tools at the storyteller's disposal.

PERCY USES these tools with equal effectiveness in two essays from *The Message in the Bottle*, "The Loss of the Creature" and "Notes for a Novel About the End of the World." As different as they are in their particulars, these two essays have in common one characteristic which is very much to the point of my argument. In each, Percy's rhetorical strategy is to "anchor" his argument in one or more images of persons in predicaments. Reminiscent of his strategy in the first half of "The

Delta Factor," this mode of argument is equally successful in these essays. Also as in "The Delta Factor" and in his first three novels, Percy's telos is to call our attention to the existential fallout precipitated by an allegiance to the Cartesian picture of the self. Once more, "little dramas of ordinary experience" are essential to the achievement of that end.

"The Loss of the Creature" opens with a reference to García López de Cárdenas, discoverer of the Grand Canyon. Percy soon discloses the nature of his interest in de Cárdenas when he observes, "Later the government set the place aside as a national park, hoping to pass along to millions the experience of Cárdenas. Does not one see the same sight from the Bright Angel Lodge that Cárdenas saw?"[15] The answer in Percy's view is probably not. Why?

> The thing is no longer the thing as it confronted the Spaniard; it is rather that which has already been formulated—by picture postcard, geography book, tourist folders, and the words *Grand Canyon*. As a result of this preformulation, the source of the sightseer's pleasure undergoes a shift. Where the wonder and delight of the Spaniard arose from his penetration of the thing itself . . . now the sightseer measures his satisfaction *by the degree to which the canyon conforms to the preformed complex.* . . . The highest point, the term of the sightseer's satisfaction, is not the sovereign discovery of the thing before him; it is rather the measuring up of the thing to the criterion of the preformed symbolic complex. (MB, 47)

Analogous to the loss which Binx speaks of in defining the malaise, this loss of sovereignty and the ontological and epistemological "shift" it embodies is the focus of Percy's attention in "The Loss of the Creature." His thesis is that this radical loss is a "consequence of the seduction of the layman by science," most conspicuous in "the caste of layman-expert," in which the layman is incapable of knowing or experiencing anything without the approving stamp of the expert (MB, 63, 54). The result, he argues, is a twofold deprivation. First, the thing itself (*e.g.*, Grand Canyon, Indian corn dance, Shakespearean sonnet) is

15. Walker Percy, *The Message in the Bottle*, 46. Subsequent references appear in the text, with the abbreviation MB.

devalued because it is so tidily "packaged." Second, the individual is himself devalued insofar as he assumes the role "not of the person but of the consumer" (MB, 54).

Percy develops his argument around three images of persons in predicaments. The first I have already mentioned. The second is of a midwestern couple who stumble upon a remote Mexican village and witness a traditional religious festival. Their delight in this discovery, however, is contaminated by a certain uneasiness dispersed only when they return later with an ethnologist friend who can "certify their experience as genuine. . . . What they want from him is not ethnological explanations; all they want is his approval" (MB, 53–54). The third predicament is that of a Scarsdale High biology student and a Sarah Lawrence English major, respectively, confronted by a dogfish and a Shakespearean sonnet. Fish and poem are "obscured" by the "educational package" in which they are presented. In each case, the student is hardpressed indeed to wrest them from these packages so that they may become something more than a mere specimen of sonnet or of dogfish; so that like the paintings in the Metropolitan, they may be seen.

Implicit in each of these scenarios are some of the same ontological and epistemological issues we have found elsewhere in Percy's work. Of special importance here is the connection he draws between the peculiar "placement" of these individuals in the world and the superordinance in our culture of theory over experience.[16] The particulars of each little drama suggest that the model of theory Percy has in mind is the regnant one. In each instance, an individual conspires in his own disenfranchisement, his own demotion, so to speak, from person to consumer. This conspiracy would not be logically possible apart from an allegiance to an account of knowing governed by the spirit of abstraction, an account which, moreover, posits reality as atemporal and independent of any person. It is this concept of reality which constitutes the logical basis of the regnant model of theory.

The decisive factor in Percy's argument in "The Loss of the Crea-

---

16. "Placement" is Percy's word and he uses it in this connection at several important junctures in his argument, a point worth remarking given the importance of the notion of "placement" in *The Last Gentleman* and in the etymology of the word *epistemology*.

ture" is that his reflections cannot be pried loose from their grounding in the concrete tokens of sightseeing, high school biology classes, and the like. At every point, he attends both *from* and *to* persons in predicaments. What he discloses in the process is that when one does otherwise—when, for example, one attends to a theory about individuals instead of to individuals themselves—a profound shift occurs in one's "placement" in the world. As Percy says at one point:

> The dogfish . . . [is] rendered invisible by a shift of reality from concrete thing to theory which Whitehead has called the fallacy of misplaced concreteness. It is the mistaking of an idea, a principle, an abstraction for the real. As a consequence of the shift, the "specimen" is seen as less real than the theory of the specimen. As Kierkegaard said, once a person is seen as a specimen of a race or a species, at that very moment he ceases to be an individual. Then there are no more individuals but only specimens. (MB, 58)

The superordinance of the theoretical over the concrete Percy describes here is precisely that epistemological situation which obtains in certain of his own essays. In them, the consequence is the same, namely, the creature, the embodied self, disappears to be replaced by the *Cogito* and the abstract tokens of Anyone, Anyplace. Yet in "The Loss of the Creature" he avoids that conceptual trap by keeping his eye firmly fixed upon persons in predicaments.

Thus once again we find that Percy's own "placement" in the world vis-à-vis his subject is contingent upon certain linguistic tokens whose bent is in this instance undeniably toward the concrete, the active, and the incarnate. As in the novels, that placement is such that he is at once constrained and empowered to expose the logical inconsistencies implicit in the dictum *Cogito, ergo sum.* In contrast, one whose placement is on the side of that dictum, so to speak, would not have at hand the conceptual tools with which to discover that therein is the creature irretrievably lost; or if by chance he did make such a discovery, it would be to him a matter of no philosophical importance.

The most complex and striking image of a person in a predicament in "Notes for a Novel About the End of the World" comes relatively late in the essay. It is the image of a scientist-technician living in the near future, by which time men have been divided into two classes, the consumer and "the stranded objectivized consciousness, a ghost of a man who wanders the earth like Ishmael" (MB, 115). Our scientist is one of the latter. Percy goes on to characterize him in such a way as to make it clear that he has equally well in hand here those epistemological and ontological issues so evident in the novels and "The Loss of the Creature":

> Unlike the consumer he knows his predicament. He is the despairing man Kierkegaard spoke of, for whom there is hope because he is aware of his despair. He is a caricature of the contemporary Cartesian man who has objectified the world and his body and sets himself over against both like the angel at the gates of Paradise. All creaturely relations crumble at his touch. He has but to utter a word—*achieving intersubjectivity, interpersonal relations, meaningful behavior*—and that which the word signifies vanishes. (MB, 115)

It would seem that this unfortunate scientist has been attacked by a veritable host of ravening particles. What will help him out of this predicament? The answer is consistent with the resolutions of both *The Moviegoer* and *Love in the Ruins*, namely, the Good News spoken with authority by a newsbearer, news which will prove apposite to the situation of him who stands in the way of hearing it.

This little drama is the centerpiece of "Notes for a Novel About the End of the World," an appropriate work with which to conclude this chapter on Percy as storyteller. In it, he reflects upon the vocation of the novelist and in particular upon that of the novelist who "has an explicit and ultimate concern with the nature of man and the nature of reality where man finds himself" (MB, 102). Such a writer, he suggests, might rightly be called a "religious" novelist. Percy uses the word *religious* here in its root sense—*i.e.*, as "signifying a radical bond as the writer sees it which connects man with reality—or the failure of such a bond—and so confers meaning to his life—or the absence of meaning." Of special concern to Percy is the function such a writer serves in modern, secular culture. At one point, he describes this function as "quasi-prophetic" and compares the novelist to a canary in a mine shaft: "The novelist is less like a prophet than he is like the canary that coal miners used to take down into the shaft to test the air.

When the canary gets unhappy, utters plaintive cries, and collapses, it may be time for the miners to surface and think things over" (MB, 101). As this splendid simile delivered in a typically sardonic tone suggests, Percy would concur with the thesis that the novelist possesses a kind of insight which distinguishes him from his fellows and issues in a singular clarity vis-à-vis the ills of modern culture. Indeed, his primary aim in this essay is to explore the nature and source of that clarity expecially as it is evident in the religious novelist. Of special interest in the present context is the implication in Percy's argument that novelists *think* in a way importantly different from the way a scientist or a sociologist thinks. This point will be the focus of my discussion.[17]

Percy opens this essay by characterizing the novelist's placement in the world in a way which must remind us of his "The Delta Factor" Martian:

> Not being called by God to be a prophet, he nevertheless pretends to a certain prescience. If he did not think he saw something other people didn't see or at least didn't pay much attention to, he would be wasting his time writing and they reading. This does not mean that he is wiser than they. Rather it might testify to a species of affliction which sets him apart and gives him an odd point of view. (MB, 101)

Like the Martian, the novelist stands apart from other men and can, therefore, see things to which they are blind. Throughout the essay Percy reiterates this point, emphasizing again and again the "oddness" of such a writer's perspective on men and society. What is significant about this Martian-novelist analogy is that here, no less than in "The Delta Factor," Percy treads a fine line between what I have characterized as appropriate versus inappropriate detachment from actors and speakers. In "The Delta Factor," as we have seen, he finally steps over the line onto the side of the latter. In "Notes for a Novel About the End of the World," however, he does not. Instead, as in his presentation of Will Barrett's unhappy aloofness, Percy is not seduced by the cult of objectivity. What seems to prevent such a capitulation is his ex-

17. Percy's list of writers who fit his definition of the religious novelist include Dostoevski, Tolstoy, Sartre, Faulkner, and Flannery O'Connor. Among those explicitly excluded are Jane Austen, Samuel Richardson, John Steinbeck, and Sinclair Lewis.

plicit reliance upon the "incarnational, historical, and predicamental" world view of Judeo-Christianity, especially insofar as he employs this view as a framework according to which he may give an account of himself as a novelist. Thus are his reflections pretended by the tokens of that very story which, he argues in "The Delta Factor," comprises the only coherent theory of man. The result is that Percy displays an extraordinary insight into the singular powers of the novelist to countermand the "schism of consciousness" which afflicts modern, Western culture.

Two passages which follow closely upon one another in the text will serve to illustrate my point. First, the crux of Percy's argument is that the novelist's "categories" are importantly different from those of either the scientist or the sociologist. How so?

> If the scientist's vocation is to clarify and simplify, it would seem that the novelist's aim is to muddy and complicate. For he knows that even the most carefully contrived questionnaire cannot discover how it really stands with the sociologist or himself. What will be left out of even the most rigorous scientific formulation is nothing else than the individual himself. And since the novelist deals first and last with individuals and the scientist treats individuals only to discover their general properties, it is the novelist's responsibility to be chary of categories and rather to focus upon the mystery, the paradox, the *openness* of an individual human existence. (MB, 108)

Implicated in this passage is the clear realization that, no matter how rigorous its application, the conceptual framework of science cannot exhaustively "accommodate" that perplexing mix of the transcendent and the immanent that is the embodied self. It cannot disclose to us what it is to be a man and to live and die.

Further—and with this, Percy puts his finger right on the heart of the matter—he also recognizes for what it is the great trap into which Tom More falls:

> For what has happened . . . is the absorption by the layman not of the scientific method but rather of the magical aura of science, whose credentials he accepts for all sectors of reality. Thus in the

lay culture of a scientific society nothing is easier than to fall prey to a kind of seduction which sunders one's very self from itself into an all-transcending "objective" consciousness and a consumer-self with a list of "needs" to be satisfied. It is this monstrous bifurcation of man into angelic and bestial components against which old theologies must be weighed before new theologies are erected. (MB, 113)

The "old theology" Percy has in mind is, as I have already indicated, that of the Judeo-Christian tradition in which man is neither angel nor beast but sovereign wayfarer; in which the world is consecrated as the locus of faith and of each man's responsibility to God and to other men. In comparison, Percy finds the new theologies to be "small potatoes indeed" and allows as how "to the 'religious' novelist, whether it be Sartre or O'Connor, the positive proposals of the new theology must sound like a set of resolutions passed by the P.T.A." (MB, 114). It is this allegiance to the Christian story of birth, death, and resurrection, and to the Hebrew one of covenant, obligation, and God's speech, together with an unflagging focus upon persons in predicaments, which serves to anchor his reflections in the human world of word and deed. The result is a lively essay in which he takes a long and very thoughtful look at the vocation of the religious novelist. Consequently, we have an excellent opportunity to "hear" a superb storyteller reflecting upon the intricacies of his craft. What he has to say suggests that so long as he intends upon that craft, so long as he "thinks novelistically," his understanding of the human creature is very rich and fraught with the possibility of further discovery.

To CLAIM that the three novels and two essays discussed here are significantly clearer and more polemically powerful than certain other of Percy's essays is not to claim that they embody a kind of perfect lucidity in the regnant, philosophical sense of that word. Nor is it to claim that the clarity of the novels and allied essays is merely a matter of their more readily yielding up certain themes or "ideas" which might be translated without loss of potency into the austere and putatively impersonal rhetoric of abstract, philosophical argument. Indeed, to make these claims would be to weaken rather than to strengthen my argument. Rather, the claim I do make is that the clarity and potency of these stories and essays is inextricably bound up with the metaphors, analogies, and rhetorical strategies which are the tools of the storyteller. That clarity and potency cannot be apart from their embodiment in the stuff of story whether that "stuff" be in a novel per se or woven into the imagery of a given essay. In both cases, the intent is the same, namely, to disclose the ills, the contradictions, the joys, and the sorrows of the human creature where and as we actually suffer them, in mind and heart, in body and spirit together; and in that compassionate disclosure, to comfort, to heal, and to rejoice.

As storyteller, Percy possesses insight into the rigors of the human condition which is informed by humor, compassion, and love. These three have no habitation apart from the mortal world. It is here and only here that the question "What does it mean to be a man and to live and die?" may be asked with any hope of an answer. It is this hope which Percy, unwittingly and to our mutual cost, surrenders when he turns to that austere and "rigorous" presentation of reality which is the highly abstract philosophical essay. In these essays, as we shall see in Chapter III, the creature so splendidly present in the novels is truly lost.

III ✦

Percy as Philosophical Essayist

OR, WHY NOVELISTS, HELEN KELLER, AND THREE-
YEAR-OLDS SUCCEED WHERE LINGUISTIC
PHILOSOPHERS FAIL

No man truly aware of his own human nature will admit that he can discover himself in the theories of modern anthropology—be they biological, psychological, sociological, or any other. Only the accidents of man—his attributes, his relations, his forms—make up these theories; they never take man simply as he is. They speak about man, but they never really see man. They approach him but they never truly find him. They handle him, but they never grip him as he actually is. . . . Forever they play out the same grotesque and fearful comedy, but its incidents strike always upon a phantom.

ROMANO GUARDINI
The End of the Modern World

The question which cannot be put off forever is not what is the nature of culture and what are the laws of culture but what is the ontological nature of the creature who makes the assertions of culture? How may we apply the scientific method in all its rigor and fruitfulness to man considered as a creature of culture? If one refuses to answer this question, one can hardly be called an anthropologist, perhaps anthropometrist, or ethnographer, but not the scientist whose business it is to know man as such. A biologist, after all, is not afraid to speak about organisms.

WALKER PERCY
"Culture: The Antinomy of the Scientific Method"

In the essays in *The Message in the Bottle* in which Percy focuses his attention directly upon the phenomenon of language—roughly the second half of the book—he dons the garb of the philosopher and launches in earnest his frontal assault on Cartesian dualism. But by his attempting to dismantle Cartesian dualism using the conceptual tools and practicing the language game of that dualism, the integrity and persuasiveness of his argument are greatly undermined. As we shall see, in each of these eight pieces—beginning with "The Mystery of Language" and ending with "Symbol as Need"—Percy is preoccupied not with persons in predicaments but rather with the development through the careful observation of symbol-mongering, of "a more radical science of man" than presently exists. Whether his immediate focus is upon semiotics, communication theory, dyadic, triadic, and tetradic models of meaning, or the act of naming—just some of the more conspicuous puzzles Percy examines

—his telos is consistent throughout, namely, "to weld the broken self whole" by applying the balm of the scientific method to the sundry hurts of humankind in the twentieth century.

If this program sounds like that of one Thomas More, M.D., the analogy is well taken and very much to the point. As we have seen, the fictional Dr. More is a man of uncommon sensitivity and insight whose radar—if I may borrow that device from Will Barrett—unfailingly zeros in on the physical and psychical ills of his fellows. Even so, More eventually goes astray, succumbing to the advances of the vaguely unpleasant but very persuasive Mr. Immelman. The works presently in question reflect a similar muddle of great insight and profound confusion on the part of philosophical essayist Percy. While the essays display an impressive familiarity with complex philosophical and linguistic issues, the integrity of such sophisticated discourse is greatly undermined when we consider the conceptual move upon which it is predicated—*i.e.*, a shift of attention from persons in predicaments to the formulation of a "radical science of man." In making this move, Percy relinquishes both the constraints and the empowerments of the storyteller's language game in favor of those which issue from that of the Cartesian philosopher. The inevitable consequence is a repetition of More's error. Percy too attempts to use the conceptual tools of a crypto-Cartesian science to remedy the shortcomings of that very science. More precisely, like Tom he subscribes to a certain second-order account of science, an account governed by the spirit of abstraction and therefore intractably bound up with the Cartesian framework. Unfolding in accordance with the indications and standards of that framework, his reflections issue in a picture of the self irretrievably abstracted from the human world of word and deed.

This phenomenon is, of course, analogous to the dissolution of Percy's argument in "The Delta Factor." In that case, the question "What sort of activity is it to devise a theory?," together with Percy's equivocal use of "theory" throughout, provided the means by which to evaluate the strengths and weaknesses of his argument. A similar line of inquiry recommends itself here as well. Although Percy's energetic pursuit of a radical science of man does not culminate until we reach the final essay in *The Message in the Bottle*, "A Theory of Language," there can be no question but that either explicitly or implicitly the term *radical science* fills the same heuristic function in these essays as does *theory* in "The Delta Factor." Moreover, Percy's development of his thesis that a more distinct understanding of language will issue in a new, radical, and unequivocally desirable "science" of man is marked by a similarly equivocal use of attendant concepts crucial to his argument—*e.g.,* "objective," "observable," "meaning," "real," "intentional," and, most important, "empirical." From this it follows that a convenient way to approach these essays would be to ask, "What does it mean to Percy to formulate a 'radical science of man'?"; and to answer that question by searching out the nature and degree of his equivocation vis-à-vis certain concepts essential to such a formulation.

If my thesis is correct, we shall find that Percy's equivocation is such as to greatly erode the coherence of his conceptual agenda. Specifically, it discloses the profound confusion which obtains when he loses his hold upon persons in predicaments and takes up instead a rhetorical posture and certain linguistic tokens which readily come to hand if one aspires, as Descartes puts it, to use his reason in all things so that his mind might "accustom itself little by little to conceive its objects more clearly and distinctly." [1] We may also find that in the context of such aspiration there is no place for a creature incapable, as Pascal says, of either certain knowledge or absolute ignorance.

IN "The Mystery of Language," Percy argues that an account of language which holds it to be merely "a series of events in space-time: muscular events in the mouth, wave events in the air, electrocolloidal events in the nerve and brain" is flawed from the outset. It is flawed because, unlike other phenomena, language "cannot be explained in the ordinary terminology of explanations"; it cannot be got hold of with the formula "Here is a phenomenon. . . . How does it work?"— the answer to which is then given as a series of space-time events. Instead, he suggests, to understand language "we must use another frame of reference and another terminology." [2] This tone of skepticism

1. René Descartes, *Discourse on Method and The Meditations,* trans. F. E. Sutcliff (Baltimore, 1968), 43.
2. Walker Percy, *The Message in the Bottle,* 151–52. Subsequent references appear in the text with the abbreviation MB.

vis-à-vis the usefulness of a narrow empirical/behaviorist approach to thinking about man as speaker is one evident not only in this essay but in others of the eight in question as well. For example, in "The Symbolic Structure of Interpersonal Process," Percy stresses the need for a "qualitative phenomenology," as distinct from a merely "quantitative science," to grasp the relation between a symbol and that which it symbolizes; in "Culture: The Antinomy of the Scientific Method," he argues that the scientific method as it is putatively practiced is inadequate as a tool with which to study what he calls "the assertory phenomena of culture"; and in both "Semiotic and a Theory of Knowledge" and "Symbol, Consciousness, and Intersubjectivity," Percy emphasizes, in a way reminiscent of Hannah Arendt's discussion of the space of appearance, the fact that all our feats of knowing require the presence of another.

In a word, it would not be overstating the case to say that the principal animus for Percy's forays into the thickets of linguistic philosophy is a healthy disrespect for the proposition that man is simply a "higher organism" and language neither more nor less than one of his more interesting and complex "behaviors"; and equally for its inverse, that man is a loose assemblage of the physical and the "mental" whose capacity for symbol-mongering rests with a mysterious language acquisition device located somewhere "in the head." These are, of course, the familiar horns of that dilemma Percy addresses in such an interestingly problematic way in "The Delta Factor." In the present context his treatment of this theme is both interesting and problematic in much the same way. Even the first-time reader of these essays must be struck with the extent to which in them, as in the latter part of "The Delta Factor," Percy's skepticism is woven into an argument which relies heavily upon a repertoire of concepts logically at odds with that skepticism. This phenomenon is perfectly illustrated in the last pages of "The Mystery of Language." In them, Percy unwittingly discloses an orientation to his subject radically different from that implicated in the novels and one which obtains in each of these eight essays.

As I have already noted, Percy begins this piece by calling attention to the fallacies of a strict empirical/behaviorist account of language. He then goes on to argue that a more fruitful approach might be to focus on the singular activity of naming and upon the difference, epistemologically speaking, between sign and symbol. His aim here is less to propound an elaborate theory about naming, signs, and symbols than it is simply to make a case for the need to think seriously about them if we are to think seriously about the nature of man and his place in the world. Certainly there is nothing controversial in this proposal. Even so, as Percy brings his argument to a close it becomes clear that his remarks are predicated upon a picture of the world unhappily consistent with that account of language he so rightly critizices early on. Specifically, after stating his assumption that we share "an empirical-realistic view of the world"—by which he means that we all believe rocks, trees, dogs, etc., exist and can be "at least partially known and partially explained by science"—he goes on to place man and language in this scheme:

> The significance of language may be approached in the following way. In our ordinary theoretical view of the world, we see it as a process, a dynamic succession of energy states. There are subatomic particles and atoms and molecules in motion; there are gaseous bodies expanding or contracting; there are inorganic elements in chemical interaction; there are organisms in contact with an environment, responding and adapting accordingly; there are animals responding to each other by means of sign behavior.
>
> This state of affairs we may think of as a number of terms in interaction, each with all the others. Each being is in the world, acting upon the world, and itself being acted upon by the world. (MB, 157)[3]

Consider carefully what Percy has done here or, perhaps more to the point, what he has *not* done. How "ordinary" is that view of the world he outlines? It is by no means ordinary in the sense of "commonsensical." Rather, the most striking thing about it is the degree to

3. Percy's proclivity for referring to the world in this abstracted way is marked in all these essays. Compare the following from "Culture: The Antinomy of the Scientific Method": "What should be noticed is that there is a difference between the sort of thing we, Scientist$_1$ and Scientist$_2$, understand the world to be (a nexus of secondary causes, event C $\rightarrow$ event E), and the assertion by which we express this understanding (E = f(C)). One is a dynamic succession of energy states, the other is an assertion, an immaterial act by which two *entia rationis* are brought into a relation of intentional identity" (MB, 236). I shall return later to the notion of a bifurcated reality implicit in this and like passages.

which it is abstracted from an ordinary/commonsensical experience of the world. The emphasis, then, must be upon "theoretical." Moreover, the appropriate sense of theoretical is clearly the regnant one, as the view of the world Percy outlines here undeniably objectifies that world, transforming it and its lively inhabitants into "a number of terms in interaction," a metamorphosis which must remind us of Helen Keller's from girl into "element."

In effect, Percy confuses an account of the world which reflects our common experience of it with one informed by exact science, the telos of which is, as Polanyi puts it, "to establish complete intellectual control over experience in terms of precise rules which can be formally set out and empirically tested."[4] The implications of this confusion should be quite clear: Percy takes as the starting point of his reflections a second-order account of reality highly abstracted from concrete experience and, as such, logically posterior to the rudimentary and commonsensical means by which we orient ourselves in the world. (Are we to believe that when Percy looks out upon a landscape of rocks and trees, he sees "a dynamic succession of energy states"? I rather suspect he sees rocks and trees.) In accepting this second-order account he moves away from his own roots in the ordinary phenomenal world, a move tantamount to choosing one framework and one set of conceptual tools—those of the exact sciences—over another framework and another set of conceptual tools—those of persons acting and speaking in a common world.

What happens next is very much like what happens in "The Delta Factor" as the result of Percy's enchantment with "the hard-headed empiricism of American behavioral scientists" (MB, 34). After outlining this "ordinary theoretical view of the world," he goes on to introduce man as "the third term" in this scheme and suggests that when this "third term" speaks and names something, it is not only unprecedented but "scandalous." He then asks the important question:

> What are the consequences for our thinking about man? There are a great many consequences, epistemological, existential, religious, psychiatric. There is space here to mention only one, the effect it has on our *minimal* concept of man. I do not mean our

4. Michael Polanyi, *Personal Knowledge* (Chicago, 1958), 18.

concept of his origin and his destiny, which is, of course, the province of religion. I mean, rather, our working concept, as our minimal working concept of water is a compound of hydrogen and oxygen. (MB, 157–58)

Percy's notion of what sort of thing a "minimal" concept of man is is very much of a piece with his "ordinary theoretical view of the world." Granted, he recognizes that the consequences of man's "scandalous" ability to name things are manifold, but whereas in the first half of "The Delta Factor" he focuses upon a *story* as a model for understanding the nature of man, here he does something quite different. Here he makes a distinction between a "religious" concept and a "minimal" or "working" concept and allies his inquiry with the latter. Further, his example of a "working" concept is strikingly reminiscent of the passage in "The Delta Factor" in which he argues that the joys and sorrows of being human can be understood as "variables" of the Delta phenomenon "just as" responses, reinforcements, etc. are "variables" of a stimulus-response phenomenon. In the present case, his example is equally revealing in that it places the "scandal" of language on the same ontological footing as $2H + \frac{1}{2}O_2 = H_2O$—and, even more to the point, posits in the model of knowing implicated in such an equation a heuristic power sufficient to illustrate the complexities of a creature who acts, speaks, hopes, and makes promises.

At this point, it might be useful to remember Will Barrett and his fine, German-made telescope—specifically, to remember that when Will purchases the telescope on the assumption that with it he can "penetrate to the very heart of things," he unwittingly chooses his weapon from the arsenal of the enemy. A telescope is, in short, the thing most likely to increase his isolation and detachment, not help him overcome them. The "purchase" essayist Percy makes in "The Mystery of Language" is very similar and, in an important sense, just as unsurprising. Like Will Barrett, Percy acts at cross-purposes with himself. In the space of a few pages he moves from an outright indictment of a narrow empirical approach to language to a tacit endorsement of an epistemology which, if followed to its logical end, would constrain its adherent to approach language in just such a narrow way. Why is this shift, which we might roughly characterize as one from common sense to scientific theory, so unsurprising? As I observed earlier, the superordination of theory over experience as the putative ground for all knowing and reflection is ubiquitous in modern Western culture. The conceptual move Percy makes in outlining an "ordinary theoretical view of the world," and then making that view the basis for an allegedly new approach to man and language, is logically of a piece with that hierarchy. Moreover, it is, as we shall see, a move he recapitulates at an ever increasing level of abstraction in each of the essays which follow "Mystery." In brief, the setting may change but the message is the same: Our everyday, commonsensical perception of and experience in the world is philosophically trivial. That which is philosophically significant is only that which may be viewed from a posture of detachment and objectivity and which is subject to proofs of a mathematical sort.

The remaining paragraphs of "The Mystery of Language" are a study in intellectual ambivalence and provide a telling conclusion to Percy's argument. After again condemning the notion that man is merely quantitatively different from other organisms, he continues:

> This happens not to be true, however, and in a way it is unfortunate. I say unfortunate because it means the shattering of the old dream of the Enlightenment—that an objective-explanatory-causal science can discover and set forth all the knowledge of which man is capable. The dream is drawing to a close. The existentialists have taught us that what man is cannot be grasped by the sciences of man. The case is rather that man's science is one of the things that man does, a mode of existence. Another mode is speech. Man is not merely a higher organism responding to and controlling his environment. He is, in Heidegger's words, that being in the world whose calling it is to find a name for Being, to give testimony to it and to provide for it a clearing. (MB, 158)

I quote the essay's concluding paragraph in full because in it the tension between the Percy who lusts after a "radical science of man" and the Percy who knows that no science modeled after the Enlightenment ideal can exhaustively interpret man to himself is very sharp. The wistfulness with which he remarks the passing of the old Enlightenment dream is especially revealing in that it discloses Percy's ambivalence toward the objectivist tradition. Clearly, there is about it something he finds very attractive. His enthusiasm for a so-called ordinary theoretical view of the world and his explicitly stated admiration for "hard-headed empiricism" suggest that in the best of all possible worlds, according to philosophical essayist Percy, the human creature would indeed be susceptible to exhaustive "explanation" according to the objective-explanatory-causal terms of the Enlightenment dream. That this is not such a world and we are not such creatures seems to be a matter of some regret to him.

It is this tone of wistfulness and regret which provides our first real clue as to what is at stake for Percy in his pursuit of a radical science of man. In "The Delta Factor" we found that, despite his recognition of its shortcomings, he continued to tinker with the behaviorist model of language in the apparent hope that it could be "fixed." In this essay and in those following, all of which antedate "The Delta Factor," we find an analogous situation. Percy is unwilling to surrender entirely the Enlightenment dream and wishes instead to "radicalize" it so that it might, he hopes, provide a framework equal to the task of disclosing who and what a man is. To put it quite simply, instead of making a truly radical conceptual move and disentangling himself from the empirical-behaviorist/mentalist-idealist bailiwick, Percy remains within its boundaries—rearranging them, it is true, but within them nonetheless.

Much, then, rides upon the notion of a "radical science of man." What exactly should such a science "look like" according to Percy? What are the criteria by which we are to judge how radical this science is? It is at this juncture that those key words I mentioned earlier become most important. In what follows I shall argue that Percy's equivocal use of these terms, each of which is "loaded" in the parlance of philosophical argument, discloses how firmly entrenched are his present reflections in the framework of Cartesianism.

It is already evident from our consideration of "The Delta Factor" and "The Mystery of Language" that "empirical" and "empiricism" figure importantly in these linguistic-philosophical essays. Indeed, it would not be exaggerating to say that one of Percy's principal aims is to demonstrate how "a broad and untrammelled empiricism" (MB, 287) is the best conceptual tool with which to probe such thorny topics as semiotics and communication theory, the difference between sign and symbol, and the relation between symbol and consciousness. Nor would it be inaccurate to take as symptomatic of the tenacity and seriousness with which Percy pursues this goal the following passage from "The Symbolic Structure of Interpersonal Process": "The embarrassing fact is that there does not exist today, as far as I am aware, a natural empirical science of symbolic behavior *as such.* Yet communication, the language event, is a real happening; it is as proper a subject for a natural science as nuclear fission or sexual reproduction" (MB, 193–94). In a word, whatever else Percy's "radical science" will be, it will most certainly be "empirical" in some fundamental and important sense.

We can begin to appreciate the implications of making empiricism, "broad and untrammelled" or otherwise, the centerpiece of such a science if we consider the conceptual company it keeps in modern philosophy. Briefly, the empirical tradition of which Locke and Hume are the progenitors is closely allied with the thesis that that which is "real" and "true" is only that which is observable and verifiable according to explicitly and proleptically formulated rules and procedures and which is, moreover, impersonal and "morally neutral" in character. Further, "verification" in this scheme is synonymous with the collection and ordering of sense data. To put the matter in rather colloquial terms, only those phenomena which lend themselves to being seen, weighed, measured, counted, put on a graph, and thus rendered (putatively) fully transparent to the observer are deemed scientifically *and therefore* philosophically important. In short, empiricism as it is commonly defined in modern philosophy sits squarely on one side of the Cartesian divide and is indispensable in the pursuit of that "complete intellectual control over experience" which is, as Polanyi argues, the avowed purpose of the exact sciences. To avoid any charge of oversimplifying this complex issue, I should quickly add there is no question but that in the eighteenth and nineteenth centuries the careful observation and recording of data, as contrasted with the pursuit of *Naturphilosophie* by Hegel and Goethe among others, played a decisive and positive role in the development of modern science. The difficulty arises, however, in the extent to which a model of knowing abstracted from the empirical method of inquiry is taken to be appropriate to all knowing and to elucidate exhaustively the nature of reality itself. Polanyi puts the fact of the matter with characteristic succinctness: "Empiricism is valid only as a maxim, the application of which itself forms a part of the art of knowing." [5]

Perhaps the one point most worth remembering here is simply that "empiricism" is an important token in the Cartesian language game. As such, it is bound up with a certain conception of reality. The question we must ask of Percy in this connection, then, is how successful is he in resisting the suasions of that conception? Does he merely rearrange the epistemology and ontology implicit in the empiricism of Locke and Hume and pushed to their logical ends in the behaviorism of B. F. Skinner? Or does Percy's empiricism offer us something new, something truly radical with which we may repudiate the conceptual strictures of Cartesianism? [6]

The passage from "The Symbolic Structure of Interpersonal Process" quoted earlier provides a convenient place to start in answering these questions. In this essay Percy examines the relationship between psychiatrist and patient as a paradigm of "interpersonal relations" and attempts to show how that relationship elucidates the incoherence of a behavioristic account of "symbolic behavior." He then goes on to argue that "a rich empirical phenomenology" will rectify this incoherence. The short paragraph above appears early in the essay and is significant in at least three respects. First, while it might be tempting to dismiss Percy's expression of embarrassment as "mere" rhetoric, to do so would be a mistake. In fact, this expression is part of an unobtrusive but sustained effort to make language and "interpersonal relations" respectable as a subject fit for "natural, empirical science." This posture in relation to science sets Percy up for an unhappy comparison with that liberal clergyman of the nineteenth century to whom he points with such irony in "Notes for a Novel About the End of the World"—*i.e.*, the one "who used to wait, hat in hand so to speak, out-

5. Ibid., 153. Consider Polanyi's entire discussion of empiricism in relation to the regnant concept of "impersonal" scientific knowledge (153–58, 167–70).

6. The only reviewer to remark Percy's equivocal use of "empiricism" is Weldon Thornton in his essay "Homo Loquens, Homo Symbolificus, Homo Sapiens: Walker Percy on Language," in Panthea Reid Broughton (ed.), *Stratagems for Being: The Art of Walker Percy* (Baton Rouge, 1979), 169–91. Thornton's remarks are quite brief (pp. 173–74) and, I think, rather inconclusive, but he does note correctly that in latching onto "empiricism" Percy does more to muddy than to clear the conceptual waters.

side the scientific laboratories to assure the scientist there was no conflict between science and religion. The latter could not have cared less." The appropriateness of this unflattering analogy becomes plain—and this is my second point—when we consider the by now familiar tactic Percy uses to ensure that respectability: "Communication, the language event, is a real happening; it is as proper a subject for a natural science as nuclear fission or sexual reproduction" (MB, 193–94). Here, just as in "The Delta Factor," it seems that for something to be judged "real" and therefore suitable as the subject of an empirical science, it must be of the same logical order as a chemical reaction or a readily observed and cataloged biological function.[7]

These two points together suggest a third. Keeping in mind the etymology of *epistemology* and the important sense in which "to know" means "to place oneself in the position required for," we may now observe that this short paragraph from "Symbolic Structure" discloses the way in which Percy places himself in the world in these essays in order to "know" man and language. In taking up the tokens of "an empirical, natural science"—including, of course, the familiar "as real as" this or that chemical/biological phenomenon—Percy takes up a certain epistemological relation to his subject just as surely as does Will Barrett when he watches his fellow museum goers from behind a pillar. In a manner of speaking, Percy's commitment to "empirical science" and his conviction that such a science promises to avoid the pitfalls of both behaviorism and mentalism is the pillar behind which he stands and which thereby governs his reflections.

The evidence that this is so and that Percy's stance may not be so different from that of a more conspicuously rigid empiricist is by no means limited to this brief passage. Rather, the ties that bind his "broad and untrammelled" empiricism to the "narrow and trammelled" sort are woven into his argument at almost every turn. Most often, this evidence takes one of two forms: either remarks disclosing approval of certain fundamental tenets of behaviorism à la George Mead and B. F. Skinner, or passages in which Percy attempts to distin-

7. Both "interpersonal relations" and "symbolic behavior" are phrases Percy uses often in this essay. "A rich empirical phenomenology" appears only once in "Symbol as Hermeneutic in Existentialism." The irony of Percy's effort to criticize a behavioristic account of what he repeatedly refers to as "symbolic *behavior*" should not pass unnoticed.

guish his own version of empiricism from the traditional one. A brief look at several instances of each will show, I believe, how heavy is his investment in an ontology and an epistemology congenial to the Cartesian mind-matter split.

I have already called attention to Percy's predilection for consistently referring to language as "symbolic behavior." His choice of words is indeed fortunate for us, in that it indicates quite plainly the repertoire of concepts which funds these reflections. In the innocuous choice to designate language as one of man's many "behaviors," Percy betrays a tacit allegiance to that reductionist picture of the self he so energetically condemns elsewhere. This reading is confirmed at several points when we find Percy granting to behaviorism a basic if limited "correctness" in his approach to the study of man. For example, he notes with approval George Mead's thesis that "an ideally refined behaviorism could explain the behavior of the observed subject" even though it must fail in explaining that of the "observing behaviorist." Later he adds, "One is still justified in calling the interpersonal process what Mead called it fifty years ago: a conversation of gesture in which my speech stimulus 'calls out a response' from you" (MB, 190, 194). Again Percy goes on to grant that saying this is not saying enough. His caveat does not, however, alter the implication that he is convinced of the fundamental correctness of the behaviorist model.

These sentiments regarding behaviorism are ones we have already uncovered in "The Delta Factor." There they were most concisely expressed in Percy's statement that even without refinement the behaviorist model is entirely adequate when applied to "the right kind of [human] behavior."[8] The point made in that connection applies equally to the present case, namely, that to concede the behaviorist model's "rightness" in this or that instance is also to concede tacitly the rightness of its basic premises and its efficacy as an instrument for reflection about the nature of man. Such a concession makes impossible any clear break with that model and all it implies about the hu-

---

8. This notion turns up over and over in all Percy's linguistic essays. See, for example, the following from "Toward a Triadic Theory of Meaning": "Even though we were not present and could not have seen the events inside Helen's head if we had been, we nevertheless feel confident that learning theory can give a fairly adequate account of the kind of events which occurred. B. F. Skinner would have no difficulty explaining what happened and most of us would find his explanation useful" (MB, 164).

man creature. The validity of this point in the present case becomes plain when we look at the section of "Symbolic Structure" subtitled "The Structure of Symbolic Behavior." In this section, Percy's well-known fondness for diagrams and arrows prevails as he develops a tetradic model of "symbolic behavior." The model, which allegedly improves upon the semiotic triangle of sign-organism-object in its addition of a second "organism," looks like this:

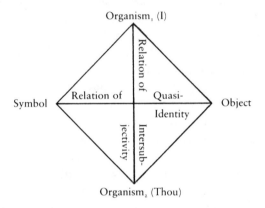

Putting aside for the moment the difficulties implicit in the ontological equality of all four "elements" of this tetrad, we find that it is here Percy introduces that notion referred to very early in his chapter—the requisite presence of the Other in all learning, knowing, and thinking.[9]

We might well be inclined to rejoice at this apparent introduction of conviviality and something akin to Arendt's space of appearance as indispensable to all our feats of knowing. Even if the neutered "elements" together with the ontological flatness of Percy's tetrad were not enough to dampen our enthusiasm, however, the paragraph which follows would surely do so:

> The new ensemble of elements and relations which comes into being does not replace but rather overlays the organismic interaction. People still interact with each other behavioristically as much

9. Percy does use the familiar "elements" here in exactly the same way as in "The Delta Factor." Cf. "Symbolic Structure" (MB, 200). Percy refers to this model again in "Symbol, Consciousness, and Intersubjectivity," "Semiotic and a Theory of Knowledge," and "Culture: The Antinomy of the Scientific Method."

as do dogs and bees, but they also enter into intersubjective relations and cointend objects through the vehicle of symbols. It is possible, and indeed preferable, to describe symbolic behavior in an
operational language which omits reference to mental contents or
even to "meanings." "Ideas" are difficult to define operationally
and even more difficult to bring into coherent relation with the
observables of behavioral science. As for "meanings," the word is
itself so ambiguous that there is more to be lost than gained from
its use. It seems least objectionable to say that in the particular
communication event under consideration, an organism intends
such and such a designatum by means of such and such a symbol.
(MB, 201)

I quote this paragraph in full because it illustrates perfectly the important point that Percy's confusion is not superficial but profound. Just
when he is on the point of introducing a truly radical notion into his
critique of the behaviorist approach to language, Percy falls back upon
the abstract language and a repertoire of concepts which are the earmarks of that approach. The entirely objectionable "elements" is still
with us, coupled this time with people who "interact . . . behavior-
istically" just like ("as real as"?) dogs and bees. The assumption that
behaviorism is fine so long as one is concerned with nothing more
than "organismic interaction" is plain. Moreover, implicit in this and
in what follows is a bifurcation of man into an "organismic" part no
different in kind from dogs and bees, and an "intersubjective" part
which traffics in symbols. The parallel with the Cartesian divide must
not pass unnoticed.

Percy's next move is even more problematic. What he means by
"operational language" is not clear, but if its chief virtue is that with it
one can avoid talking about "meanings," then it must be putatively
impersonal and value-free. We can assume, moreover, that with it we
could not speak of certain troublesome things which distinguish us
from dogs and bees—*e.g.*, willing, hoping, and the telling and understanding of stories. What are we to make of Percy's preference for such
a language? First, it is significant that he lumps "meanings" with
"mental contents" and "Ideas" and rejects all three because they do
not conform to the "observables" of behavioral science. Percy does not

explicitly define "observable," but we may assume he means that which is coterminus with one or more of our five senses. In short, he executes the classic behaviorist move, rejecting as "ambiguous" all that does not conform to the standards of "as real as." [10] Second, implicit in the suggestion that we could in fact have an "operational" language in which "meanings" could be separated out like the yolk of an egg, is a very odd notion of what constitutes meaning in the first place. Are we to assume that as "elements and relations . . . overlay . . . organismic interaction," meaning "overlays" certain parts or facets of life but not others; that it can be lifted off or separated out, leaving something "observable" that is tidily unambiguous and meaning-free? Such a conception could only be predicated upon a mind-body dualism in which "meaning" is relegated to one or the other side of a great divide, synonymous with "mental contents" on the one hand and on the other obviated entirely, replaced by the putatively neutral observation and cataloging of "data." [11]

Finally, what of Percy's "least objectionable" alternative to "ambiguous" talk about meaning, ideas, and the like? It is if nothing else a study in abstraction and, as such, logically of a piece with what precedes it. Notice in particular that "communication event," "organism," and "designatum" have taken the place of more homely words such as "speech" or "conversation," "person," and "subject" or "topic of conversation." To what purpose is this substitution made? Is this an example of "operational language"? The answer to neither question is very clear. What is clear, however, is that such language does not lend itself to thinking and talking about persons in predicaments. In making himself its advocate, Percy sets himself at great distance from any world inhabited by a creature so unruly and "ambiguous" as ever to find himself in—to put it plainly—a mess.

Percy's tetrad and his gloss on it are of central importance in his case against a behavioristic theory of "interpersonal process." For that

10. This is not the only time Percy makes this move. Earlier he uncritically dismisses any concern with "ideas," "thoughts," and "feelings" as part of "the old mentalist nightmare." It is, he says, "the altogether praiseworthy objective of the behaviorist" to get beyond this nightmare. Cf. MB, 195.

11. This conception of meaning is also implicit and equally problematic in Percy's distinction between sign and symbol. I shall return to this issue shortly.

reason, the strong intimations in this section that his argument unfolds according to the suasions and pretensions of Cartesian dualism are indeed revelatory. The important question remaining is, how does this "ensemble of elements and relations," together with a call for "operational language," translate into an empirical science? Does what Percy has to say about this science confirm or contradict the thesis that it is logically of a piece with the dualism implicit in his tetrad? What we shall find, I think, is that Percy's remarks about an empirical science per se reflect precisely the same confusion as we have already discovered in his references, explicit and oblique, to behaviorism.

Early on in this piece, Percy describes the business of empirical science as being "to investigate phenomena as they happen." He then specifies, "The real task is how to study symbolic behavior, not formally by the deductive sciences which specify rules for the use of symbols in logic and calculi, but empirically as a kind of event which takes place in the same public domain as learning behavior." This approach to the study of "symbolic behavior" is supposed to provide a third alternative to "a behavioristic theory of meaning, the energy exchange bouncing back and forth between speaker and hearer like a tennis ball" and "the old miraculous mind reading by means of words." Whether his approach will issue in such an alternative is doubtful, however. Our first clue that something is amiss is his positing a common "domain" for "symbolic behavior" and "learning behavior." Percy uses the latter term in the usual behavioristic sense to denote, for example, the "learning" exhibited by Pavlov's well-known and long-suffering dogs and, putatively, by Helen Keller before her discovery at the well house. By so casually and uncritically introducing this problematic notion at this juncture in his argument, Percy says more than he knows. First, his remark suggests that he either does not recognize or chooses to ignore the poverty of this notion in its application to human beings. Second, by placing these two "behaviors" under one roof, Percy invites us to ask, in what sense are they alike such that they share a common domain? Is "symbolic behavior" subject to the same rules of observation and verification as "learning behavior"? Percy does not raise, much less answer, these questions. Finally, by setting both "symbolic behavior" and "learning behavior" in their "public domain" over against the presumably "private domain" of the deductive sciences, Percy does not abrogate the either/or choice between "observables" and "mental contents"; instead, he perpetuates it.

All that is troublesome about the above passage turns up again and very soon in the course of Percy's argument. He begins the section "Some Molar Traits of the Communication Event" with the observation, "The fact is that the generic traits of symbolic behavior are not 'mental' at all. They are empirically ascertainable and have indeed been observed often enough" (MB, 195–96). Putting aside the interesting question of what constitutes a "molar trait," we might more profitably ask what Percy means by "generic trait" and "empirically ascertainable." By the former, he apparently means the basic ingredients, so to speak, of "symbolic behavior," and he gives us three examples: the dyadic or two-person structure of interpersonal relation (Jurgen Ruesch and Joseph Jaffe); "autonomous object interest" among children (Ernest Schachtel); and the concepts of distance and relation (Martin Buber). While Percy discusses the first two only briefly, he goes on at some length about the third, and in a most telling way. Even though he acknowledges distance and relation as being "of the utmost relevance to the basic structure of symbolic behavior," he is clearly sympathetic to the social scientist's suspicion of the framework out of which Buber develops these concepts, namely, that of philosophical anthropology. In particular, he notes that these "traits" are expressed "as modes peculiar to human existence rather than as directly observable features of human relations . . . [and as such] they must strike the empirical scientist as vague in meaning and difficult to define operationally" (MB, 197).[12]

Not only is Percy sympathetic to this critique of philosophical anthropology but, perhaps more importantly, he is at pains to argue that his own empirical approach will eliminate the difficulties in the analysis of "symbolic behavior." Moreover, his new science will eliminate

---

12. Percy himself places Schachtel's phrase in quotes and both *distance* and *relation* are italicized in the text. Percy has more to say about Buber later and it is along the same line. "The distinction between *Welt* and *Umwelt* has been made before. Buber characterizes man as the creature who has a world and sets it at a distance, beyond the operation of his drives and needs. But, insightful as such an observation may be, it is of doubtful value to the behavioral sciences until it can be grounded in a coherent theory of symbolic behavior" (MB, 204).

these problems insofar as it accommodates the model of clarity and rules of verification implicit in the empiricist's objections. This spirit of accommodation is quite plain when he applies his critique of Buber reflexively to the "traits" contributed by all four, Buber, Schachtel, Ruesch, and Jaffe:

> What is more important, these traits are ascertainable not by a philosophical anthropology—which source is itself enough to render them suspect in the eyes of the behavioral scientists—but by an empirical analysis of language events as they are found to occur in the genetic appearance of language in the encultured child, in blind deaf-mutes, and in the structure of everyday language exchanges. (MB, 197)[13]

In effect, given the choice between a philosophical anthropology and the "operational" approach of behavioral science, Percy unambiguously weighs his own approach on the side of the latter. Predictably, however, he goes on to argue that in fact his proposal does not represent one side of an either/or choice—which he characterizes as one between American positivists and European existentialists—but offers a third alternative: "Surely the better course is an allegiance to the empirical method—but not, let me carefully note, an allegiance to a theoretical commitment" (MB, 198). The "but not" is of the greatest importance here for it uncovers what may be Percy's chief weakness as a thinker. He begins this essay by deploring the divorce between theory and practice which prevails in psychiatry and in social psychology. Nevertheless, the cornerstone of his own alternative is *just such a divorce*. To put it plainly, Percy presumes to isolate the "method" of empiricism from its "theory" and thereby escape the confines of a rigid behavioristic approach to man and language. This is to say, he presumes that action (practice) and reflection (theory) are logically heterogeneous and, as such, can be quite casually disconnected from one another. This presumption is as thoroughly flawed as is the Cartesian bifurcation of thinking thing and extended thing which is its antecedent.

13. Here, as in the long passage following Percy's diagram, it is worth noting the ease with which he falls into the highly abstract vocabulary of social science—*e.g.*, "everyday language exchanges" is apparently deemed better, more "precise" perhaps, than "ordinary conversation."

If there is any lingering doubt as to the validity of my point, then consider one final brief passage from this essay:

> It should be emphasized that this empirical approach does not require the settling or even the raising of the question of the ontological status of the intersubjective relation. The latter is introduced as a postulate which is valid to the extent that it unites random observations and opens productive avenues of inquiry. (MB, 202)[14]

This little paragraph is remarkable in at least two respects. First, Percy repeats his "but not" move in a form even more damaging than the original. Implicit in his remark is the thesis that any "ontological" issue is beyond the pale of the empiricist, who must confine himself strictly to what is "observable" and "ascertainable" by the empirical method; or to put it differently, he must limit himself to establishing a "minimal" or "working" concept of man. This is to accord to "ontology" the same treatment meted out earlier to "meaning." It is, in a word, to suggest that the study of man's words and deeds, spoken and acted in a common, public world, have no important and *irreducible* connection to his "being" and that the empiricist is thereby free of any responsibility to elucidate that connection.

Second, for sheer opacity the next sentence may be unequaled in all of Percy's work. In this it follows logically upon the former, breezily reducing the whole issue of ontology to a mere "postulate" designed to "unite random observations" and "open productive avenues of inquiry." What does this mean? It would be very hard to say. This fact is in itself noteworthy, however, in that it calls attention to how disconnected is Percy—and by implication, how disconnected is his "empirical approach"—from the mundane world of actors and speakers. Sounding exactly like those scientists in *Love in the Ruins* who suffer from chronic angelism and whose spirits roam the world like

14. Percy makes an almost identical move in regard to "the ontological status of the coupler" at the close of "A Theory of Language." I shall return to this in Chapter V. See also a passage from "Culture" which similarly attests to Percy's wish to eliminate ontological issues from these reflections about man and language: "The argument which follows precinds from an explicit philosophy of science. It does not matter for a moment what one believes the ontological character of the scientific statement to be, as long as one admits it to be a statement" (MB, 215).

Ishmael, Percy bears unwitting testimony to the consequences of trying to make man over into what he is not, either an angel or a beast.

Percy's enchantment with empiricism and the host of conceptual difficulties which issue from that enchantment are paradigmatically expressed in "The Symbolic Structure of Interpersonal Process." In each of the remaining essays in this group, these difficulties are equally in evidence, as we shall see in the remainder of this chapter. The first part of the concluding section will treat, with relative brevity, four of the remaining six essays: "Semiotic and a Theory of Knowledge," "Symbol, Consciousness, and Intersubjectivity," "Symbol as Hermeneutic in Existentialism," and "Symbol as Need." The focus of this section will be upon Percy's persistent prejudice in favor of an empirical/behaviorist approach to language. In the final part, I shall look at "Culture: The Antinomy of the Scientific Method" and "Toward a Triadic Theory of Meaning," giving special attention to the last section of each essay.

THROUGHOUT OUR consideration of "The Symbolic Structure of Interpersonal Process" and "The Mystery of Language," I held that Percy's preoccupation with a "radical science of man" and in particular his insistence that that science be fundamentally "empirical" betray a significant indebtedness to the framework and conceptual tools of Cartesianism. Further, I suggested that Percy's putatively new empiricism is predicated upon a divorce of theory and practice reminiscent of Descartes' distinction between *res cogitans* and *res extensa*, a predication most clearly revealed in the crucial "but not." We must now look at a few key passages from each of four essays, all of which attest that this is not a passing conceptual fancy on Percy's part but is rather a persistent theme and one central to his argument in each of these pieces, no matter what the specific focus of his attention. In addition, these passages will illustrate Percy's continued equivocation vis-à-vis those concepts essential to the formulation of his "radical science."

Apart from its initial appearance in "Symbolic Structure," the "but not" move is perhaps nowhere more plainly in evidence than in the opening pages of "Symbol, Consciousness, and Intersubjectivity." In this essay, Percy discusses two very different approaches to the study of consciousness, namely, "the explanatory-psychological" as represented by George Mead and "the phenomenological" as represented by Edmund Husserl. He faults both for their inability to take proper account of "intersubjectivity, that meeting of minds by which two selves take each other's meaning with reference to the same object held in common" (MB, 265). Percy's way of filling this lacuna is, not surprisingly, to make a distinction between sign and symbol and to examine "two characteristics of the symbol meaning-relation, *as they are empirically ascertainable*, which distinguish it from the sign relation" (MB, 269). These are the tetradic structure of the former (the same tetrad which appeared in "Symbolic Structure") and the necessity for two "organisms" as the prerequisite for "symbolization."

Percy's aim here is entirely commendable, namely, to rescue the symbol from the rigid stimulus-response framework of behaviorism on the one hand and from the abstraction of transcendental phenomenology on the other. He proposes to do so by calling attention to the necessary presence of "a real or posited *someone else*" as the "*enduring condition*" upon which the meaning of a symbol of any sort—in language, art, thought—is contingent. From there, he goes on to argue that consciousness itself is both intentional and symbolic in character. So what is the trouble here? Early on, Percy admits to a certain "prejudice" in favor of Mead's approach to consciousness and then adds: "If Mead's social behaviorism is too narrow a theoretical base, it can be broadened without losing the posture from which Mead theorized, that of an observer confronting data which he can make some sense of and of which he can speak to other observers" (MB, 267). Consider carefully what Percy proposes here. The "posture" from which Mead develops his social behaviorism is an irrefutably Cartesian one. That is, his is the posture of an "objective" observer, one who sets himself-as-knower over against the world-as-object. He is, in Percy's own words, "an observer confronting data." This bloodless image is in itself quite telling, as with this single stroke Percy reveals his argument to be funded by a repertoire of concepts which reduces actors and speakers to mere "data" to be observed in a detached and noncommittal way.[15]

15. The reason Percy gives for being prejudiced in Mead's favor is, in itself, telling: "I am frank to confess a prejudice in favor of Mead's approach to consciousness as a

As Percy's argument progresses, this repertoire of concepts intrudes itself again and again. Suggesting "from the objective-empirical point of view" that we may study consciousness "as we study anything else"—*i.e.*, as we study any "empirically ascertainable" phenomenon—he then proceeds to refer consistently to "organisms" rather than to "men," "persons," or "human beings." Just as "element" is inappropriate in connection with Helen Keller, Percy's preference here for "organism" strikes a jarring note as part of a model of consciousness which allegedly offers an alternative to both a reductionistic behaviorism and an isolate, discarnate transcendentalism. The effect is constantly to remind us that Percy's posture is just what he says it is, that of an "observer confronting data." This posture and the concepts attendant upon it, set side by side with Percy's repeated avowal to go between the horns of the behaviorist/mentalist dilemma, comprise a perplexing tangle of movements and countermovements. Most perplexing and most problematic of all is his firm conviction that he can with impunity abstract behaviorist theory from behaviorist practice and make this feat the basis of his "radical science"; or to put it in a different and frankly indecorous way, his conviction that he can lie down with behaviorist dogs and not get up with a few Skinnerian fleas. In the present context, this tangle catches at the feet of his sure instinct that "consciousness" is neither strictly private (Husserl) nor merely the product of social conditioning (Mead). The result is a model of consciousness requiring two "organisms" and dependent for its cogency upon "an impartial empirical analysis" of "symbolization." The result, in short, is a model of consciousness not *radically* different from Husserl's and Mead's.

The nonradical nature of Percy's argument in "Symbol, Consciousness, and Intersubjectivity" is characteristic of his argument in each of

---

phenomenon arising from the social matrix through language. It seems to me that the psychological approach possesses the saving virtue that it tends to be self-corrective, whereas in transcendental phenomenology everything is risked on a single methodological cast at the outset, the famous *epoché*" (MB, 266). Though Percy goes on to point out certain limitations to Mead's approach, he does not explain how it is "self-correcting." Consider also the following from "Toward a Triadic Theory of Meaning": "What would happen if we took [Charles] Peirce seriously? That is to say, if we retain the posture of behavioral science which interests itself only in the overt behavior of other organisms, what are we to make of observable behavior which cannot be understood as a series of dyadic energy transactions?" (MB, 162).

these essays. In "Semiotic and a Theory of Knowledge" he proposes to undertake an "open" semiotical analysis of symbolization, "one undertaken without theoretical presuppositions." The telos of this undertaking is to show that "a true 'semiotic,' far from being the *coup de grâce* of metaphysics, may prove of immense value, inasmuch as it validates and illumines a classical metaphysical relation [between symbol and object]—*and this at an empirical level*" (MB, 245).[16] Percy's development of this thesis hinges upon a distinction between sign and symbol about which two points need to be made. First, a sign according to Percy merely "points" while a symbol "means." Second, the relation between a sign and that to which it points is "real" while the relation between a symbol and that which it symbolizes is "intentional." Now, at this juncture we must recall the highly problematic treatment accorded "meaning" in "Symbolic Structure." In that context, Percy identified "meaning" with "mental contents" and displayed the uneasiness characteristic of the classical empiricist before any such notion. This indentification, I argued, is itself logically homogeneous with a prior bifurcation of man into an "organismic" part and an "intersubjective" part analogous to Descartes' extended thing and thinking thing respectively. Significantly, his distinction between sign and symbol follows these same lines. Turning once again to his favorite example, Helen Keller, he points to her discovery at the well house as embodying the difference between the two: "Is her joy a 'hallucinatory need-satisfaction,' an atavism of primitive word-magic; or is it simply a purely cognitive joy oriented toward being and its validation through the symbol?" (MB, 260). What bears remarking here are the either/or choices Percy consistently puts before us: either atavistic "word-magic" or "pure" cognition; either an "organismic" function or an "intersubjective" one; either pointing and a "real" relation or meaning and an "intentional" relation. This either/or formula is significant not only because each "side" is roughly analogous to one or the other side of the Cartesian divide. Even more important is the radical demarcation of reality into two parts: that in which the issue of "meaning" does not exist and that in which the issue of "meaning" is paramount.

16. He later claims that his inquiry is "purely empirical" and therefore "free of the dogmatic limits of positivism" (MB, 258).

To illustrate my point, let us look briefly at Percy's use of "real" and "intentional" in distinguishing between sign and symbol. According to Percy, the relation, "A causes B," is a "real" or sign-relation; "A names B" is an "intentional" or symbol-relation. The former, he argues, is dyadic, exists quite apart from any observer or interpreter, and is therefore antecedent to the problem of meaning. The latter is triadic, requires the presence of an observer or interpreter and is therefore synonymous with the problem of meaning.[17] This is to claim that before her discovery at the well house when Helen Keller reached for a piece of cake after Miss Sullivan spelled c-a-k-e in her hand, this gesture was merely the expression of a "real" relation in which the concepts "meaning" and "intentionality" have no place. To make such a claim is, quite simply, to forget that the assertion "A causes B" must be made *by someone*; that no relations "real" or otherwise exist *as such* in the natural world apart from the intentional consciousness which names them. It is, to put it another way, to forget that the connection made between c-a-k-e and something good to eat requires the heuristic power of a sentient, intentional consciousness even though it may be a rudimentary one.

Thus to distinguish between "real" on the one hand and "intentional" and "meaning" on the other is to do at least two things. First, it is to suggest that neither meaning nor consciousness are rooted in our prelinguistic mind-bodies. Rather, both are synonymous with "mental contents" and radically disjunct from our merely physical ("organismic") selves which are able, we must suppose, to traffic in nothing but "causal" relationships; able only, in short, to behave. The second point follows from the first. Percy's real/intentional distinction betrays his inability, persistent in these essays, to think in terms other than ones governed by the Cartesian framework. Here in relation to man we have but a variation on the theme of man-as-angel or man-as-beast. Worth remarking in this connection are Percy's scattered references to the pre-discovery Helen Keller as "a sign-using animal."

17. In "Symbol as Need" Percy puts it concisely: "Signs announce their objects. Thunder announces rain. The bell announces food to Pavlov's dogs. When I say James to a dog, he *looks* for James; when I say James to you, you say, 'What about him?'—you *think* about James" (MB, 292). I should add here that Percy vacillates between a triadic model of the symbol-relation and a tetradic one. The salient features of sign/symbol, real/intentional distinction are consistent, however.

Moreover, this radical bifurcation rends not only man but all of nature. That is, nature is putatively transparent and the study of it held to be immune to the vagaries of the student. As Percy says in "Symbol as Hermeneutic in Existentialism," "If there is an unresolved dualism of questioner-and-nature in the professed monism of the empiricist, its difficulties do not become apparent as long as the questions are asked of nature" (MB, 277).[18] In other words, "real" relations obtain in the natural world and are presumed to be liable of presuppositionless and value-free study. Only when we turn to man himself and "intentional" relations are our reflections apt to be less than perfectly "clear" in the regnant sense of the word—and this difficulty could *in theory* be obviated if only we had a sufficiently "radical" science of man (if only we had the right semiotic, the right model of "symbolization" with the right number of "organisms" engaging in "intersubjective" behavior). So goes the argument of essayist Percy.

By now the conceptual difficulties attendant upon Percy's pursuit of "a radical science of man" should be very plain. There remains only to bring this discussion to an end by looking at two dense though relatively brief parts of the essays "Culture: The Antimony of the Scientific Method" and "Toward a Triadic Theory of Meaning." I conclude with these two because in the former Percy addresses the difficulty of applying the scientific method to the study of "man himself in his distinctive activity as a culture member" (MB, 239); and in the latter assesses the value of the alternative, a "novelistic" approach to the study of man.

In "Culture: The Antimony of the Scientific Method" Percy argues that the Achilles' heel of the scientific method shows itself when that method is applied reflexively to itself:

> The ineluctable reality upon which the scientific method founders and splits into an antinomy is nothing else than the central act of science, "sciencing," the assertions of science. . . . It is ironical but perhaps not unfitting that science, undertaken as a total organon of

18. He makes a similar point in "Culture": "A chemist or a biologist is not faced with a normative variable in the data" (MB, 241). What Percy overlooks is that a "normative" variable is never "in the data" but is "in the scientist." Indeed, in an important sense, the "data" is "in the scientist" as well.

reality, should break down not at the microcosmic or macrocosmic limits of the universe but in the attempt to grasp itself. (MB, 233)

This passage introduces a line of argument which addresses in a way more direct than any we have previously encountered the question I posed early on in this chapter, namely, what, according to Percy, should a radical science "look like"? What has been problematic all along, of course, is the clear indication that what he has to propose is fundamentally nonradical; moreover, it is nonradical in a way consistent with the uncritical appropriation of a certain second-order account of what scientists do and how they do it. In Percy's distinction between "real" and "intentional," we have had intimations of this fatal flaw in his "radical science"—*i.e.*, in the bifurcation of reality into the "meaning-free" and the "meaning-ful." The passage above brings us at last to the heart of the matter: Percy fails to make the all-important distinction between the actual practice of scientific inquiry in which hunches, guesses, and other indecorous phenomena are indispensable and the regnant, second-order account of such inquiry which conceives natural science as "a set of statements which is 'objective' in the sense that its substance is entirely determined by observation even while its presentation may be shaped by convention."[19] Not only does Percy fail to make this distinction, but implicit in all these essays is an endorsement of this conception. The caveat that "the scientific method" breaks down "in the attempt to grasp itself" does not in any way mitigate that endorsement but only underscores the flaw in Percy's argument. He does not recognize that "the scientific method *never works*—not in the study of ion exchanges, the feeding habits of amoebas, or the mental disorders of men—it never works as the objectivist tradition suggests, devoid of any acts of appraisal, any personal participation, any active responsibility on the part of the scientist/ knower. Percy is quite persistent, however, in his belief that just such putatively impersonal knowledge is not only possible but desirable in the study of the natural world. Further, as his argument in "Culture" makes clear, he is convinced that if a sufficiently rigorous version of the scientific method ("rigorous" in the objectivist sense of the word)

19. Polanyi, *Personal Knowledge*, 16.

were applied to the study of man and culture, the notorious opacity of both might be rendered transparent.

Percy's argument along these lines comes to a head in the final section of "Culture" subtitled "Toward a Radical Anthropology." It is well worth remarking in this connection that the quotation used as an epigraph to this chapter comes from this section and the choice was, of course, quite deliberate. In a clear and concise way, it illustrates perfectly the extent to which Percy's response to the failure of science vis-à-vis the study of man is to make that science even more "scientific." What follows underscores this point:

> The answer, I think, is not to be found in a limitation or compromise of the scientific method but rather in making it a more radically useful instrument. To return to the tetradic structure of the scientific enterprise: a radical science must be willing to admit as eligible phenomena all real events, not merely space-time linkages. It must deal with assertory behavior as such; it cannot disqualify as a datum the very phenomenon of which it is itself a mode. (MB, 239–40)

Not only should the familiar tokens "eligible phenomena," "assertory behavior," "space-time linkages," and "datum" warn us that we are still dealing with the conceptual framework which issued in Mead's speech-as-stimulus and Schactel's odious "autonomous object interest," not to mention Percy's own "element" and "organism," but the "tetradic structure" imputed to this science (the same atemporal and ontologically flat tetrad we see elsewhere) makes it clear that the conceptual difficulties which plague other essays in this group are with us still. To put the matter quite plainly, a "radical anthropology" which is to "take account of ontological levels more radical than the scope of the functional method" will inevitably fail in its purpose if modeled upon a "radical science" that is atemporal and characterized by an unyielding ontological monism.

The irony of this impasse in which Percy pits himself against himself is accentuated in his treatment of the "novelistic alternative" in "Toward a Triadic Theory of Meaning," the final section of which is subtitled "The Lady Novelist: A Tertium Quid?" In this essay, Percy outlines "a theory of language as behavior based upon Charles Peirce's distinction between "two kinds of natural phenomena," so-called dyadic and triadic relations. The phrase "language as *behavior*" gives a clear indication of what Percy is about here. His hope, he declares, is that this theory "might either stimulate or irritate behavioral scientists toward the end that they will devise operational means of confirming or disconfirming these statements—or perhaps even launch more fruitful studies than this very tentative inquiry" (MB, 160).

In order to achieve this end, Percy believes he must "disentangle from Peirce's metaphysic those insights which are germane to a view of language as behavior"—*i.e.*, he must separate a theory of reality from a theory of language. Why he must is not clear, but after a lengthy and strenuous effort to do so in which he offers "a loose set of postulates . . . suitable for a behavioral schema of symbol use," we come to the essay's final section. Here Percy poses the following question:

> So here is the real question, or rather the main specter which haunts every inquiry into language as behavior. Granted the shortcomings of the two major methodological approaches to the talking patient—the analytic-psychical and the organismic-behavioristic—is not the sole remaining alternative the novelistic? (MB, 186)

His answer, of course, is "No"; that "a genuine triadic theory" of "triadic behavior" could do an equally good job of elucidating the anxiety of a patient talking to his therapist. "Such a theory," he argues, "might bestow order and system upon the phenomenologizing which to the behavioral scientist must seem closer to novel writing than to a science of behavior" (MB, 187). What is striking about this section is Percy's suspicion that the "lady novelist" may in fact possess a certain power of insight denied the behavioral scientist, set over against his conviction that the "right" behavioral science ("a genuine triadic theory") will prove that scientist every bit the novelist's equal. To concede otherwise would be, as he puts it, to concede that "all the fun [has] gone out of the game of behavioral science and the scientific method [has] itself lost its splendid rigor." In effect, Percy is determined to deny that any instrument of reflection is superior to that of the behavioral scientist when it comes to thinking about man. For him, it is a question of "rigor," and clearly the lady novelist eavesdropping on patient and psychiatrist does not measure up; therefore, her method of inquiry must be judged inferior to the scientist's.[20]

Once again, it seems, Percy's prejudice for the "scientific" has the upper hand in his argument. How are we to settle this issue? Percy settles it for us, though in a way other than he might wish. One of the most incisive and funniest episodes in *Love in the Ruins* occurs early in the novel when one Ted Tennis comes to visit Dr. More. He is suffering an advanced case of angelism compounded by impotence. His symptoms, which he recites "with precision and objectivity," include the inability to say, simply, that he loves his wife (he feels "considerable warmth and tenderness" toward her); sundry musings about the "etiology" of impotence to which he refers as an inability to "achieve an adequate response"; and a fervent wish to "restore [his relationship with his wife] along the entire spectrum." More realizes that Ted Tennis "has so abstracted himself from himself and from the world around him, seeing things as theories and himself as a shadow, that he cannot, so to speak, reenter the lovely, ordinary world. Instead, he haunts the earth and himself" (LR, 32–34). Convinced that the only treatment for such excessive abstraction is recovery of the self through ordeal, More prescribes not the "Bayonne-Rayon training member" Ted requests but a hike home through the snake and alligator infested swamp: "So it came to pass that half-dead and stinking like a catfish, he fell into the arms of his good wife, Tanya, and made lusty love to her for the rest of the night" (LR, 37).

Now, compare the flesh and blood vividness and compassionate humor of this scene with the following account à la "a genuine triadic theory" of a patient in a similar situation:

> The patient's agitation is not dyadic misery—resistance to the disclosure of unacceptable unconscious contents—but triadic delight. This delight, moreover, is quite as fundamental a trait of triadic behavior as organismic "need-satisfaction" is in dyadic behavior. It is a naming delight which derives from the patient's discovery

20. The relation of psychiatrist-patient is one Percy uses throughout this essay, as he does elsewhere as a model of language as behavior. The "rigor" he has in mind here is again that imputed to the scientist in the objectivist tradition—a rigor which exists, as I have argued after Polanyi, only in the Cartesian *Cogito*.

that his own behavior, which until now he had taken to be the unformulable, literally unspeakable, vagary of one's self, has turned out not merely to be formulable, that is to say, nameable by a theory to which both patient and therapist subscribe, but to be nameable with a name which is above all names: *oedipal*! (MB, 187–88)[21]

In what way is the coldness and abstraction of the above an "improvement" over the concreteness and compassion of the novelist's depiction of patient and therapist? The judgment that it is an improvement could be made only by one cut off from his roots in the ordinary world in which ordinary people feel pain, anger, anxiety, and joy. Such folk do not, I suspect, feel "a naming delight" any more than they engage in "everyday language exchanges" in lieu of conversations or see "a dynamic succession of energy states" when they look out their front doors. In short, Percy's response to the challenge of the lady novelist is to retreat to a presumably safe distance from the world she portrays and interpose between it and himself "a genuine triadic theory" of "triadic behavior." In this it is logically of a piece with each of the essays we have examined in this chapter.

AT THE CLOSE of Chapter II, I suggested that the creature so splendidly present in the material considered there would be absent from the essays to be examined in Chapter III. We have found this to be so. Even those shades of the human creature which do occasionally appear—*e.g.*, the patient and therapist in "Toward a Triadic Theory of Meaning"—are so immured in the abstract discourse of the philosopher-linguist-scientist as to be barely visible or, perhaps more to the point, barely audible.

How are we to account for this metamorphosis in the reflections of one very sophisticated and very thoughtful writer? The answer lies, I believe, in just this absence from these arguments of persons in predicaments. When the territory of the imagination is thus bereft of human inhabitants, that space must necessarily be filled with some other shape. Given our philosophic tradition, it should not be surprising

21. It is worth remembering that "*oedipal*" has no meaning apart from the *story* of Oedipus who killed his father, married his mother, et cetera. I would also call the reader's attention to the strong similarity between Percy's abstract language here and that of Ted Tennis in his conversation with Tom More.

that that "other" appears as an abstraction bearing little resemblance to any familiar, creaturely form. What is surprising and equally instructive, however, is that the latter springs whole, like Minerva, from the head of one who in another time and in another ontological and epistemological "place" regards it with the irony and the healthy disrespect it deserves. Thus do we find ourselves with an antinomy more complex than that of which Percy writes in "Culture: The Antinomy of the Scientific Method," one which rends the very heart of our culture and our selves.

Yet for all his sometime obsession with "science," "rigor," and the "empirically ascertainable," Percy is still a master storyteller. It is to that Percy to whom we must now return, not in the context of a story per se but rather in the context of yet another essay, "The Message in the Bottle." There, in the image of the castaway awaiting news from across the sea, storyteller Percy speaks to the plight of the broken self in a voice philosopher Percy would be unable to hear.

IV ❧

"The Message in the Bottle"

OR, WHAT IT MEANS TO BE A CASTAWAY AND WAIT
FOR NEWS FROM ACROSS THE SEAS

The act of faith consists essentially in knowledge and there we find its formal or specific perfection.
THOMAS AQUINAS
De Veritate

Faith is not a form of knowledge; for all knowledge is either knowledge of the eternal, excluding the temporal and the historical as indifferent, or it is pure historical knowledge. No knowledge can have for its object the absurdity that the eternal is the historical.
SØREN KIERKEGAARD
Philosophical Fragments

But what if it should be the case that [the castaway's] symptoms of homelessness or anxiety do not have their roots in this or that lack of knowledge or this or that malfunction which he may suffer as an islander but rather in the very fact that he is a castaway and that as such he stands not in the way of one who requires a piece of island knowledge or a technique of island treatment or this or that island need satisfaction but stands rather in the way of one who is waiting for a piece of news from across the seas?
WALKER PERCY
"The Message in the Bottle"

IN CHAPTER III, we focused upon the implications of a shift in Percy's attention from persons in predicaments to the formulation of "a radical science of man." In "The Message in the Bottle," we find that shift reversed and his attention fixed upon the castaway, a person in a very grave predicament indeed. Perhaps the most important consequence of this reversal is that Percy recovers that which he relinquished in the problematic linguistic essays, namely, the constraints and empowerments of storytelling. This recovery is crucial to the clarity and persuasiveness of his argument that our form of discourse and our way of knowing and being are congruent and cannot be abstracted from one another.

No less than the essays studied in Chapter III, "The Message in the Bottle" is about these three: language, knowing, and being. Most important, it is about the irreducible connection between them. The presumption that this radical bond exists *together* with the story of the castaway sets this essay apart from the linguistic pieces. In the latter, Percy is at pains to purge from his reflections questions bearing upon the ontological status of *Homo loquens, Homo symbolificus.* Equally banished are persons in predicaments. Instead, he limits his inquiry to the "operational" and "empirically ascertainable." In "The Message in the Bottle," however, these issues are paramount and find their perfect embodiment in the story of the castaway.

We already know the castaway to be an important token in Percy's effort to answer the question "Why is man so sad in the twentieth century?" For him the man cast up on an unfamiliar shore, amnesiac and thus bereft even of his own name, is a paradigm for the denizen of this age, who likewise has no name. In "The Message in the Bottle" Percy turns again to this image. This time the conceptual work required of our nameless but undaunted hero is sustained and complex. As we shall see, the man who awaits the newsbearer serves a heuristic function analogous to that of "theory" in "The Delta Factor" and "radical science" in the linguistic essays. The results are importantly different, however—a discrepancy which should prove most illuminating.

These issues are not new. In this chapter, as in the first three, our focus will be upon the felicity of Percy's critique of Cartesian ontology and epistemology relative to the form in which that critique is presented. Even so, "The Message in the Bottle" provides a new and very useful perspective on this issue. In it, Percy argues that one may adopt different "postures" relative to any given sentence.[1] He goes on to suggest that the posture one does in fact adopt is bound up with his situation in the world, together with the mode in which the sentence is presented; or as he puts it toward the end of the essay, together with the bearing and authority of the newsbearer. This is to say that, if the castaway does not "stand in the way of hearing news," he will be deaf to the message of the newsbearer. Conversely, if the newsbearer does not speak with authority and directly to the predicament of the castaway, his words will rightly go unheeded.

Implicit in this relation between castaway and newsbearer is the thesis that our feats of knowing are rooted in the concrete particulars

1. "Posture" is Percy's word and he uses it in this connection throughout the essay. It is of special importance in the section "The Posture of the Reader of the Sentence" in the essay "The Message in the Bottle." I shall return to this point later.

of our own history, that they require an act of appraisal on the part of the knower, and that they are profoundly convivial. We have only to remember the first half of "The Delta Factor" or Will Barrett watching the world from behind a pillar—watching and barely surviving attack by the ravening particles—to realize that this notion is one central to all of Percy's best work. Its development in "The Message in the Bottle" is worth special attention for at least two reasons. First, this thesis "surfaces" to a degree heretofore unseen as Percy focuses upon the onto-epistemic posture of the castaway relative to differrent "categories of communication" (MB, 140).[2] Not only must we be struck by this sudden lack of reticence in the face of such "ambiguous" issues but, in addition, must account for why, *contra* "The Delta Factor," his argument does not dissolve into behavioristic jargon punctuated by triangles, arrows, and the like. Second, Percy brings these reflections to bear upon what is surely the most vexed issues in Western epistemology, the relation between faith and reason. Using the category of "news" as distinct from "knowledge *sub specie aeternitatis,*" he argues that only a radically new model of knowing and not some reworking of a Thomistic, Kierkegaardian, or Hegelian model—much less a behavioristic one—fits the task of answering the question "What is it to be a man and to live and die?" Moreover, the model of knowing implicated in the category "news from across the seas," as distinct from "island news," cannot be abstracted from the *story* of the castaway. Thus not only does Percy recognize the need for a radically new approach to these complex issues, but that recognition is itself pretended by a story; and the rudimentary model he goes on to propose bears a reflexive relation to that story.

LIKE THAT OF "The Delta Factor," the opening of "The Message in the Bottle" is "neither a Skinnerian nor a Chomskian one." "Suppose," Percy begins, "a man is a castaway on an island." He goes on to say that the castaway in question lost his memory when shipwrecked;

2. In a way which will become clear later in this chapter, Percy's "categories" are closely allied to the respective provinces of the genius and the apostle as Kierkegaard defines them in *On the Difference Between a Genius and an Apostle.* In an interview published in 1974, Percy said of the work that it was for him "the most important single piece Kierkegaard wrote." See Bradley R. Dewey, "Walker Percy Talks about Kierkegaard: An Annotated Interview," *Journal of Religion,* LIV (July, 1974), 284.

that he is "a resourceful fellow" who makes the best of a bad situation, settling in to become "a useful member of the community"; and finally, that he enjoys walking on the beach, which is littered with bottles washed up from the sea, each carefully corked and containing a brief message. His only immediate problem seems to be how to classify these messages which are of several sorts. For example:

> Lead melts at 330 degrees.
> The market for eggs in Bora Bora [a neighboring island]
>   is very good.
> If water John brick is.
> In 1943, the Russians murdered 10,000 Polish officers
>   in the Katyn forest.
> Tears, idle tears, I know not what they mean.
> A war party is approaching from Bora Bora.
> Being comprises essence and existence. (MB, 120–21)

What does Percy accomplish with this introduction? First, the initial "Suppose . . ." sets a convivial tone in a way reminiscent of "Why . . . ?" in "The Delta Factor." The effect is the same—*i.e.*, to invite the reader to engage actively in reflection rather than be the passive recipient of an edifying discourse. Second, the brief but vivid scenario which follows puts before us a man who, despite the fact that he recovers sufficiently from shipwreck to become "a useful member of the community," is nonetheless a castaway who does not know his own name. This simple, inescapable fact lies at the heart of his new life. Thus Percy not only establishes as the locus of his interest a person in a predicament (another point of comparison with "The Delta Factor") but, in addition, calls attention to a significant lacuna in that person's story which no amount of resourcefulness can fill. Quite simply, the castaway's true identity, signified by his proper name, can never be inferred from the particulars of his island life. That knowledge is held by one across the sea.[3]

Finally, there are the messages themselves. They are an eclectic lot and provide no ready answer to the questions which naturally arise for

---

3. Hugh Kenner, "On Man the Sad Talker," *National Review*, XXVII (September 12, 1975), 1000.

the castaway and his fellows: "How shall we go about sorting the messages? Which are important and which are not? Which are more important and which less?" Thus the messages not only prompt the castaway to take action in the form of sorting but, more important, require that he develop criteria according to which the relative significance of the messages may be determined and the sorting accomplished.

These three points together indicate the bent of the entire essay. From the beginning, Percy attends *from* a person in a predicament *to* a person in a predicament and invites his reader to do the same. As in "The Delta Factor" he eschews the tokens and rhetoric of abstract philosophical argument in favor of the concrete tokens and convivial tone of the storyteller. In contrast to the linguistic essays, it is the latter which comprise the conceptual framework of these present reflections. We have seen elsewhere that this choice of framework is by no means an indifferent matter, and "The Message in the Bottle" is no exception.

One detail about the person and predicament from and to which Percy attends here is especially important: At no point in the essay does "the castaway" acquire a proper name. Moreover, the fact of his namelessness is important to the way he sorts the messages on the beach. Just how important is not immediately apparent. What is apparent, however, is that the castaway's criteria are based upon something other than "conventional practice," according to which the sentences would be divided into two groups, those which "appear to state empirical facts which can only be arrived at by observation . . . [and those which] seem to refer to a state of affairs implicit in the very nature of reality (or some would say in the very structure of consciousness)"—*e.g.*, "Chicago is on Lake Michigan" and "$2 + 2 = 4$" respectively. In the castaway's view, this conventional classification is unsatisfactory because it fails to distinguish between "those messages which are of consequence for life on the island and those messages which are not." By contrast his own standard of judgment would be based upon just this distinction:

> To the castaway it seems obvious that a radical classification of the sentences cannot abstract from the concrete situation in which one finds oneself. He is as interested as the scientist in arriving at a

rigorous and valid classification. . . . But he insists that the classification be radical enough to take account of the hearer of the news, of the difference between a true piece of news which is not important and a true piece of news which is important. (MB, 124)

Even expressed in this brief and rudimentary way, it is clear that the epistemology implied in the castaway's posture is radical indeed. The conventional distinction presupposes that the knower-as-subject assumes a posture of detachment over against the world-as-object, a posture which putatively affords him perfect lucidity. From this benighted point of view he performs experiments, makes statements, and writes sentences which like-minded men either assent to or challenge from an equally disinterested perspective. This posture and this activity Percy places under the rubric of "science" in the broad sense of *Wissenschaft* and suggests that its pursuit is not limited to natural scientists per se. Rather, it may include artists, poets, and philosophers (indeed!) as well.[4]

What the castaway proposes flies in the face of this model at every point. First, he recognizes for what it is the determined insularity of those who insist that "this very special posture of 'science' . . . is the only attitude that yields significant sentences." Moreover, he notes that "people who discover how to strike this attitude of 'science' seem also to decide at the same time that they will only admit as significant those sentences which have been written by others who have struck the same attitude" (MB, 123–24). What is especially important about the castaway's acuity here is that this is the very "attitude" Percy himself adopts in the essays examined in Chapter III. His obsession with "science," "rigor," and the "empirically ascertainable," together with this insistence that only in the scientific method do we have the means to solve the puzzle of who and what a man is, provides a perfect example of the intellectual monism the castaway rightly abjures. It should not pass unnoticed that once again Percy acknowledges the limitations of a position he embraces with enthusiasm elsewhere—"elsewhere" de-

---

4. *Wissenschaft* is the word Kierkegaard uses consistently and with the same intent in *On the Difference Between a Genius and an Apostle*. See the translator's note in *The Present Age* and *On the Difference Between a Genius and an Apostle*, trans. Alexander Dru (New York, 1962), 89.

noting not merely other works but, most important, another conceptual framework and language game.

Second, by emphasizing the importance of his "situation," the castaway confers upon the world a status it lacks when viewed from the posture of science. This point is crucial if we are to understand how radical is the epistemology implicit in the castaway's modest proposal. In effect, by making his situation central to the castaway's appraisal of the messages, Percy quietly introduces and acknowledges as philosophically significant all that is implicated in that situation. And what is that? It is, of course, the stuff of drama and narrative—*i.e.*, persons, action, intention, conflict, and resolution. This familiar array of tokens determines the castaway's stance in relation to the messages and provides the tools with which he hopes to interpret them. Thus does the stuff of stories enter into what may be Percy's most radical work. It is certainly the one in which he is most adroit at turning the essay form to some end other than one consonant with the night exaltations and morning terrors of a closet behaviorist.

At this early stage in the essay we have only intimations of these things to come. Even so, these intimations are enough to make it clear that Percy is transacting serious business here and has only begun to disclose the conceptual richness of the castaway's predicament. The remainder of "The Message in the Bottle" is devoted to this disclosure and focuses upon the difference between "knowledge" ("science" in the above sense) and "news." Specifically, Percy distinguishes between three categories of communication, "knowledge *sub specie aeternitatis*, "island news," and "news from across the seas." Each has its own constraints and empowerments, its own verification procedures and canons of acceptance. Most important, to take up any one of these three, the castaway must place himself in a certain position or assume a certain posture in relation to the world. Thus we might observe at the outset that knowledge *sub specie aeternitatis*, island news, and news from across the seas are not ontologically and epistemologically neutral. On the contrary, each is intentional and stretches the self in a distinctive way. The last, however, has special heuristic potency in relation to the castaway's predicament. How and why this is so—its implications vis-à-vis an alternative to the conventional distinction between faith and reason and, subsequently, a new way to think about the Christian gospel—will be the focus of the rest of this chapter.

IT WILL BE useful at this point to remember a scene from *The Moviegoer* in which Binx recalls the days when he lived in his room as "an Anyone living Anywhere" and read only "fundamental" books. At the time of this recollection, he has long since gotten onto the search and sees the fallacy of his old program: "The only difficulty was that though the universe had been disposed of, I myself was left over." Binx's recollection is germane here because the subject of the so-called fundamental books is what the castaway calls knowledge *sub specie aeternitatis*—i.e., "knowledge which can be arrived at anywhere, by anyone, and at any time" (MB, 125). For example, the claims "Lead melts at 330 degrees" and "Men should not kill each other" both fall into this category, because they express knowledge which can *in theory* be arrived at by any person on any island at any time.

This analogy between Binx reading his fundamental books and a scientist in pursuit of knowledge *sub specie aeternitatis* serves to elucidate the claim made earlier that Percy's three categories of communication, of which knowledge *sub specie aeternitatis* is one, are not ontologically and epistemologically "neutral." In this connection two points must be made, the first concerning Binx's and the scientist's "posture" in relation to the knowledge they respectively seek, and the second concerning the model of truth implied in that seeking.

When he reads fundamental books, Binx's relation to the world is analogous to that of the Cartesian philosopher-observer. As he puts it, "I stood outside the universe and sought to understand it." We know the consequences: the application to all things the criteria appropriate to the knowledge of Anyone, Anyplace; thus will he *not* stand in the way of hearing news.

What are the scientist's criteria? In the present context, two points are especially important and fall under the headings "The Scale of Significance" and "Canons of Acceptance." As to the first, Percy observes: "The scale of significance by which the scientist evaluates the sentences in the bottles may be said to range from the particular to the general. The movement of science is toward unity through abstraction, toward formulae and principles which embrace an ever greater number of particular instances" (MB, 130–31). We must be reminded here of Percy's remark in "The Delta Factor" that the spirit of the old modern age informed by the spirit of abstraction "could not address one single word to [a man] as an individual self but could address him only as he resembled other selves" (MB, 26). It is this impetus toward abstraction and consequent prejudice in favor of the general and theoretical at the expense of the particular and concrete which Percy has in mind here. The point is the same: While this "scale of significance" might be useful in evaluating, say, the accuracy of Mendeleev's law of periodicity or the unified field theory—*i.e.*, appropriate to the pursuit of knowledge *sub specie aeternitatis*—it is of no use whatever in resolving the predicament of the castaway; it cannot tell him who he is or where home is.

The second point under "Canons of Acceptance" has to do with the problem of verification. How does the scientist decide to accept or reject a piece of knowledge *sub specie aeternitatis*? Percy argues that acceptance is "synonymous with the procedure of verification." This procedure may take the form of "experimental operations, deductions, or interior recognition and assent to the truth of [a given] statement" (MB, 133). In each instance, however, acceptance or rejection depends upon the application of certain proleptically determined and putatively impersonal rules and procedures. Any sentence, any knowledge claim which fails to meet this standard of verification or which has significance only insofar as it bears directly upon the castaway's life will be regarded as nothing more than "empirical observations of a random order" and, at best, relegated to "the lowest rung of scientific significance [as] the particular instances from which hypotheses and theories are drawn" (MB, 128).

These two points, together with Percy's discussion of the posture of objectivity, indicate very clearly the conceptual territory occupied by knowledge *sub specie aeternitatis*. The epistemological values implicit in this category of communication are synonymous with those implicit in the second half of "The Delta Factor" and in the essays examined in Chapter III. In particular, the emphasis upon the detachment of the knower from the known places knowledge *sub specie aeternitatis* squarely in the Cartesian epistemological camp. What, though, of the ontology implicit in this category? A way of knowing is necessarily allied to a way of being, and the epistemology implied in knowledge *sub specie aeternitatis* is no exception. Once again Binx provides the key.

The point at which Binx's fundamental books fail him has nothing to do with the accuracy or inaccuracy of the theories they present. Whether or not *The Expanding Universe* gives a correct account of interstellar physics is of no importance. Rather, his problem is logically anterior to any such question; *The Expanding Universe* can tell him nothing about what it means to be a man and to live and die. Its silence on this subject is logically consistent with the aspiration to, as Binx puts it, "dispose of the universe." The writer and the reader of so-called fundamental books must be intent upon one thing only, Absolute Truth. No less than does Plato's philosopher-king, he seeks truth that is immune to the vagaries of time and individual knowers, truth that transcends all historical particularities. Insofar as a man sets his sights upon this absolute truth he must conform his being to the requirements of its pursuit. He must do as Binx does, stand outside the universe and seek to understand it, abstracting his feats of knowing from the particularities of his own situation. He must, in short, resemble as closely as possible the Cartesian *Cogito*.

Thus does the reading of fundamental books presuppose not only a model of truth fashioned after the veracity of a mathematical equation but an ontology consonant with that model as well. This model of truth and its allied ontology equally obtain in the category knowledge *sub specie aeternitatis*. Perhaps the single best indication that this is the case falls under the heading "Response of the Reader of the Sentence":

The appropriate response of the reader of a sentence conveying a piece of knowledge . . . is to know this and more. . . . The man who finds the bottle on the beach and who reads its message conveying a piece of knowledge undertakes his quest, verification and extension of the knowledge, on his own island or on any island at any time. His quest takes place *sub specie aeternitatis* and, in so far as he is a scientist, he does not care who he is, where he is, or what his predicament may be. (MB, 137)

Unlike news, the hearing of which issues in action, knowledge *sub specie aeternitatis* issues in "the verification and extension of the knowledge"—*i.e.*, more knowledge of an increasingly abstract and theoretical sort. Moreover, so clamant is this telos that it informs the whole of the scientist's life and being. Thus is his world constituted; thus is he himself constituted. In the end he no longer even notices that he is a castaway on an island and does not know who he is or where home is. If the newsbearer arrived and offered answers to these questions, he would surely dismiss them as philosophically and scientifically trivial. After all, what can a man's name tell us about the expanding universe?

Early in this chapter I observed that "The Message in the Bottle" is about the irreducible connection between language, knowing, and being. In his discussion of knowledge *sub specie aeternitatis*, Percy elucidates the nature of that connection by showing how a given framework and language game—in this case that of *Wissenschaft*—provides a habitation for the self at once shaping and being shaped by it. As a category of communication, knowledge *sub specie aeternitatis* bears just such a reflexive relation to the scientist-knower. Perhaps most important, however, is Percy's point that while one framework may disclose the secrets of the expanding universe, it is powerless to do work of a very different sort—*i.e.*, to answer Binx's perennial question. Moreover, if that framework is forced upon that question or vice versa, then the puzzle of who and what a man is becomes merely one more piece in the puzzle *sub specie aeternitatis* of the expanding universe. As Percy puts it, "once a piece of news is subject to the verification procedures of a piece of knowledge, it simply ceases to be news" (MB, 133). Thus is the identity of the castaway in danger of being irretrievably lost.

For the present, however, knowledge *sub specie aeternitatis* will not have the last word. Percy's exegesis of "news," and particularly of "news from across the seas," outlines a radical alternative to the ontoepistemic values implicit in knowledge *sub specie aeternitatis*, an alternative as different from the latter as is, say, *Love in the Ruins* from "Culture: The Antinomy of the Scientific Method." This analogy is, in fact, very much to the point. As we shall see, the conceptual territory occupied by news from across the sea bears a striking resemblance to the neighborhood of drama and narrative. With this inviting prospect in mind, we may return to the castaway busily sorting messages.

Unlike the scientist, the castaway is preeminently "a man who finds himself in a certain situation." And "to say this is practically equivalent, life being what it is, to saying that he finds himself to be in a certain predicament" (MB, 128). It may actually be misleading to say "unlike the scientist," because he too is almost certainly in a predicament. The difference between him and the castaway—and all else follows from this—is that if the scientist is aware of his predicament he shows no interest in it; for the castaway, his predicament is the center of his life. This seemingly innocuous contrast serves Percy as a point of departure in developing his second category of communication, news. In contrast to knowledge *sub specie aeternitatis*, news will tell the castaway nothing about Mendeleev's table of periodicity or the unified field theory. It will not even tell him that men should not kill one another. What it may in fact tell him is who he is and where home is.

We are already acquainted with the fundamental difference between knowledge and news. While the former is the province of Anyone, Anyplace and allied to the pursuit of Absolute Truth, the latter has meaning only in the context of one man's predicament. This basic distinction spills over into more specific points of contrast. For example, whereas the posture of the scientist-knower is that of objectivity—*i.e.*, a relation of detachment and standing-over-against—the posture of the castaway is that of a man who knows himself to be in trouble, is therefore attentive to his immediate circumstances, and is always on the alert for some sign of that which will deliver him. Whereas the scale of significance appropriate to knowledge *sub specie aeternitatis* is "the scientific scale of particular-general," that appropriate to news is simply its "degree of relevance for [the castaway's] predicament." Whereas the canons of acceptance for a piece of knowledge are synonymous with certain rules and procedures of verification, those for a piece of news are its relevance to one's predicament, the "credentials" of the newsbearer, and the possibility of the news (that it is neither patently false nor of an "unheralded, absurd, or otherwise inappropriate character"). Finally, whereas knowledge *sub specie aeternitatis* issues in more of the same, news issues in action—specifically action appropriate to one's predicament.

These points make plain the gulf that separates knowledge and news as categories of communication. Most important, however, is what we can infer from them as to the conceptual territory occupied by news. Earlier, I argued that in making the castaway's situation pre-eminent in his classification of the messages, Percy unobtrusively but unequivocally confers upon the stuff of that situation—persons, action, intention, conflict, and resolution—a significance it lacks under the rubric of science. We may now enlarge upon this point by noting that other allied concepts are woven into his elaboration of this theme. One deserves special comment and that is the notion of conviviality.

In discussing the credentials of the newsbearer, Percy underscores the importance of his reputation or "mien" and the necessity that he speak "with perfect sobriety and with every outward sign of good faith," so that his message will be taken seriously. He then continues:

> The message in the bottle, then, is not sufficient credential in itself as a piece of news. It is sufficient credential in itself as a piece of knowledge, for the scientist has only to test it and does not care who wrote it or whether the writer was sober or in good faith. *But a piece of news requires that there be a newsbearer.* The sentence written on a piece of paper in the bottle is sufficient if it is a piece of knowledge but it is hardly sufficient if it is a piece of news. (MB, 136)

In short, the category news *cannot be* apart from the relation that obtains between castaway and newsbearer, any more than it can exist apart from the singular predicament of the castaway. For his part the newsbearer must deliver his message with sobriety and in good faith; the castaway must in return make an appraisal of both bearer and message. It is only at the juncture of these two that news has life and reality.

If this line of argument reminds us of a point made in Chapter I, then we are right on target: The speaking and hearing of news constitutes a polis; the pursuit and capture of knowledge *sub specie aeternitatis* does not. To make this claim is to claim in part that, unlike the truth of the latter, the truth of news is dramatic and agonistic; it cannot be apart from the space of appearance created when one person speaks and another listens and speaks in turn. It is also to claim that the veracity of news, like that of the coherent theory of man of which Percy writes in "The Delta Factor," is not an atemporal, once-and-for-all affair. Rather it must be constituted anew each time the newsbearer speaks and the castaway hears. Third, it is to claim for news as a category of communication the singular power attributed by Hannah Arendt to the polis—*i.e.*, it is the "place" in which a man may most fully appear and in which he is most fully human; the only place in which who he is may be revealed.

This analogy between news and the polis discloses the profundity of the difference between knowledge and news. To put the matter in the familiar idiom of Polanyi and Wittgenstein, the framework and language game of news are radically different from those of knowledge *sub specie aeternitatis*. That difference is such as to ally the former with story, with action, with the alternative models of theory and truth outlined in Chapter I—in short, with a host of concepts logically at odds with the Cartesian framework. All these Percy puts to work in the essay's final section, "The Difference Between Island News and News from Across the Seas." There the issues implicit in the story of the castaway come together in his critique of Kierkegaard's response to Hegel on the nature of religious belief.

For the purposes of this discussion, we need not dwell for long on the category island news. By island news Percy simply means news which bears upon some specific need—biological, social, economic, etc. For example, to a man dying of thirst the news that there is water over the next hill is news indeed and he would do well to pay attention. Island news is, in brief, "news relevant to the castaway's survival as an organism, his life as a father and husband, as a member of a culture, as an economic man, and so on." Such news has great bearing upon his life but does not assuage his sense that "something is wrong . . . something is missing" (MB, 143).

The castaway knows that neither island knowledge nor island news can even reveal what that "something" is, much less correct or provide it. His predicament defies such remedies because it is, ultimately, an ontological one. Quite apart from this or that "need satisfaction," he is: "not in the world as a swallow is in the world, as an organism which is what it is, never more or less. Our islander may choose his mode of being. . . . But however he chooses to exist, he is in the last analysis a castaway, a stranger who is in the world but who is not at home in the world" (MB, 142). What then must he do? He must not, Percy argues, pretend to be at home when he knows himself to be otherwise. To do so would be a sign of despair. Instead, he must search for news from across the seas. This is not to say he should abandon all parts of his island life save combing the beach, but he must, like Binx Bolling and Tom More, learn to watch and to wait and to listen; he must "live in hope that such a message will come."

As the reference to Binx and Tom should remind us, this is a familiar scenario. In their cases the story stops just short of revealing the particulars of the message each awaits. "The Message in the Bottle" stops at this point as well, as Percy again wisely refuses the role of newsbearer. What he does do, however, is to suggest that the news which can come only from across the sea—the message of the apostle in Kierkegaard's language—is in the sphere of the transcendent, while both island news and knowledge *sub specie aeternitatis*—the message of the genius—are in the sphere of the immanent.[5] What does this mean and what has it to do with the castaway? Specifically, what has it to do with the felicity of the castaway's story as an instrument for reflection, one with which to think about the Christian gospel?

As we have seen, news is logically akin to the polis and as such occupies the same conceptual territory as drama and narrative. With this point in hand we must recall another made in Chapter I, namely, that the superiority of drama and novel as media for a theory of man is in large part due to the tension between transcendence and immanence embodied in them, a tension which has its analogue in ourselves *qua* selves. Now, the castaway's predicament is not that he lacks this or that bit of knowledge but that he lacks a name. And what, as the bard asked, is in a name? Folded into a proper name are both the specifiable particulars of a person's history *and* the ultimate opacity of that history, the "I" not equal to the sum of any particulars. Hence, a name

---

5. Percy follows Kierkegaard closely here in his distinction between the genius and the apostle and their respective spheres of the immanent and the transcendent. Cf. especially Kierkegaard, *On the Difference Between a Genius and an Apostle*, 90–91.

signifies the complex union of immanence and transcendence which together make the self a self. We might say, then, that the castaway's difficulty is that he has been deprived of that transcendent part of himself signified by the name he has lost and is thereby cast away amongst particularities. Although his island and his life there sustain him in many good and necessary ways, that sustenance is incomplete. Just as Binx and Kate discover the limits of "flesh poor flesh," discover that the body cannot of itself sustain them either singly or together as selves, so too does the castaway discover that even if one's island is beautiful it is not enough.

This is not to say that if the newsbearer appears and tells the castaway who he is and where home is he will be rendered transparent to himself and feel completely at home on his island. Indeed, such a transformation would be antithetical to the special nature of the message, as it would be tantamount to transforming news into knowledge. Rather, what will happen is that the castaway's opacity to himself will be transformed from a blank, a zero, into that which frees him from necessity, that which imbues his island life with substance and meaning, that which reconciles him to himself. This transformation will be the castaway's salvation. After a long period of wandering in the wilderness he will come home—only to find that home *is* the wilderness, transformed by the water of God's speech sprung from the lips of the newsbearer. It cannot be otherwise.

Kierkegaard too knew that salvation comes only by news, only by hearing. But, as Percy very shrewdly observes, in his attempt to rescue Christianity from the Hegelians Kierkegaard abandoned the radical implications of this insight and joined battle with Hegel on the latter's own turf. As Percy puts it:

> Kierkegaard recognized the unique character of the Christian gospel but, rather than see it as a piece of bona fide news delivered by a newsbearer, albeit news of divine origin . . . he felt obliged to set it over against knowledge as paradox. . . . Kierkegaard may have turned his dialectic against the Hegelian system, but he continued to appraise the gospel from the posture of the Hegelian scientist—and pronounced it absurd that a man's eternal happiness should depend not on knowledge *sub specie aeternitatis* but on a piece of news from across the seas. (MB, 147)

Percy's insight here is most important, not only for what it says about Kierkegaard but also for what it says about Percy and his preoccupation with news and knowledge as categories of communication. It is clear that he recognizes how seductive even for so powerful and innovative a thinker as Kierkegaard are the familiar categories and conceptual tools which readily come to hand in a discussion of faith and reason, knowledge and belief, and what these have to do with the special character of the Christian gospel. At the crucial point, Kierkegaard embraces the conceptual strictures placed upon Christianity by Hegel, a move evident in the high value he places upon the "absurdity" that "the Maker of man was made man that the ruler of the stars might suck at the breast"; the "absurdity" that "in Him the Flesh is united to the Word without magical transformation . . . in Him the Word is united to the Flesh without loss of perfection."[6] By so doing, Kierkegaard tacitly conforms his own reflections to the Hegelian hierarchy which ranks "historical" knowledge very low, knowledge *sub specie aeternitatis* very high, and accords to faith no place at all. Within this framework, reason and faith can never meet.

In developing the notion of news as a category of communication, Percy seeks to avoid Kierkegaard's error by providing a new way to think about these complex issues, a way which does not tacitly acquiesce to the conventional distinctions between faith and reason, knowledge and belief. Rudimentary as his alternative is, I believe he succeeds; or more precisely, I believe he is "onto something" of great promise. With the castaway and his singular predicament firmly in hand, Percy circumvents the old categories and suggests instead that we must take seriously the notion that salvation comes by hearing and that it "happens" on our very ordinary island. Far from requiring us to put aside our island life, it redeems that life, even as the Flesh was redeemed when in the person of Jesus of Nazareth it became one with the Word. By "take seriously" I mean, and I think Percy means, simply that we must attend to these rudiments of our hope in a way commensurate to what they are, namely, logically and existentially anterior to the arts of *Wissenschaft*.

Finally, the categories knowledge and news bear an important re-

6. St. Augustine, *An Augustine Synthesis*, ed. and trans. Erich Przwara (New York, 1945), 180–81; W. H. Auden, *For the Time Being: A Christmas Oratorio*, in *Collected Longer Poems* (New York, 1969), 182–83.

flexive relation to Percy's own work and to the thesis of this essay. What he devises in "The Message in the Bottle" is nothing less than a powerful tool for distinguishing between the constraints and empowerments which accrue to the postures of the philosopher-essayist and the storyteller-novelist respectively; or in the idiom of Chapter I, between a theory of man modeled after the regnant understanding of theory and one modeled upon an understanding of theory drawn from storytelling. The special usefulness of this tool lies in the extent to which it enables us to see why the latter (storyteller-as-theorist) is in a better position to answer Binx's and Kierkegaard's question than is the former. The most convincing proof that this is the case lies with Percy himself. As we shall see in Chapter V, no sooner does he turn back to the highly abstract mode of the philosophical essay than the lesson of "The Message in the Bottle" is lost upon him who fashioned it. What should properly be the subject of news and bodied forth in the language game of the storyteller toward the end of easing the castaway's predicament is transformed into an object of knowledge abstracted from any familiar world and made to serve the dubious end of a "radical science" or, even worse, a "semiotics of the self."[7]

To put the matter simply, when in "A Theory of Language" Percy gives himself over to the exigencies of dealing with linguists on their own turf and in their own language, he forgets the one thing the castaway must never forget: He is a castaway first and last and, as such, must stand ready to hear news from across the sea. All else—all action, all knowledge, all love—follows from this. He must remember; otherwise the castaway is lost to himself and his island becomes his prison.

KNOWING AS we do the unhappy bent of the linguistic essays, we must appreciate all the more Percy's resistance in "The Message in the Bottle" to the suasions of abstract philosophical argument. The logical dominance of the castaway constitutes the heart of that resistance. In this and in his consequent distinction between knowledge *sub specie aeternitatis*, island news, and news from across the sea, Percy supports

7. This phrase is Percy's and appears in Linda Whitney Hobson's "The Study of Consciousness: An Interview with Walker Percy," *Georgia Review*, XXXV (Spring, 1981), 60.

the point made early on in this essay regarding the intentionality of literary forms and the singular heuristic power of the storyteller. While he makes his case in rather different terms, the point is finally the same: The rhetorical stance one adopts in relation to a given question or issue is not indifferent. A given stance, or "posture" as Percy calls it, will be felicitous in one instance and infelicitous in another. Further, this state of affairs is not merely "academic" but has profound implications as to the onto-epistemic status of the person-as-knower.

That Percy argues this point at all is significant. What is more important, however, is the conceptual alliance between news and story on the one hand and knowledge *sub specie aeternitatis* and the philosophical essay on the other. I have argued that drama or narrative—story in the most fundamental sense—is the medium most likely to yield a coherent theory of man. Abstract philosophical argument, however, is the medium most likely to distort our picture of the self stretching it into disparate parts, all-seeing *Cogito* and dumb, insensate flesh. Percy effectively makes the same point when he argues that, for all its virtues, knowledge *sub specie aeternitatis*, the proper subject of the philosophical essay, is unsuited to answering the question "what is it to be a man and to live and die?" This question, he suggests, is properly the subject of news—which is to say, properly the subject of story.

This is not to say that, as Percy defines it, news from across the sea is synonymous with story. The former is a very special story; indeed, the paradigm for all stories in the de facto Christian West. It is to suggest, however, that in these latter days when it seems unlikely a newsbearer will appear bringing news "of divine origin," it may be that the storyteller—if he learns to watch and to wait and to listen—may serve after John the Baptist as one who makes the way for Him whose coming is promised.

V ᵛ

The Joys and Sorrows of Symbol-Mongering

OR, WHY IT IS BETTER TO STAY IN COVINGTON,
LOUISIANA, AND WRITE STORIES THAN VENTURE
TO M.I.T. AND BE CAPTURED BY A LANGUAGE
ACQUISITION DEVICE

What do I believe? As a philosopher, I would seem especially equipped to give an answer here, and yet my profession may be just the thing that screens me off from the human intent that lies behind the question. A philosopher may be able to reel off his ideas by the yard and yet remain blind to the things that really keep him going in life.

WILLIAM BARRETT
The Illusion of Technique

It is an inevitable consequence of an incoherent theory that its adherents in one sense profess it—what else can they profess?—yet in another sense feel themselves curiously suspended, footing lost and having no purchase for taking action. Attempts to move issue in paradoxical countermovements. As time goes on, one's professed view has less and less to do with what one feels, how one acts and understands oneself.

WALKER PERCY
"The Delta Factor"

A picture held us captive. And we could not get outside it, for it lay in our language and language seemed to repeat it to us inexorably.

LUDWIG WITTGENSTEIN
Philosophical Investigations

IN AN INTERVIEW published in 1981, Percy was asked if there were anything he regretted not having done. He answered, "I think if I were doing it all over again, I would study linguistics because it is going to be the new science." As if this declaration were not disquieting enough, he elaborates by introducing a thesis we know to be fraught with conceptual difficulties, namely, that a "radical science" as distinct from our "magnificent, triumphant . . . [but] nonradical science" will disclose to us "what it is to be a human being, to find oneself in human predicaments." Here Percy identifies this so-called radical science with semiotics and adds, "I'm sure that the human experience cannot be reduced to any science but you need a way of thinking about all these situations I write about and other novelists write about. . . . There should be a way of thinking about these things rationally."

Semiotics in the form of a "semiotics of the self" will presumably provide this "rational" approach.[1]

Although the principal works to be taken up in this final chapter are "A Theory of Language," *Lancelot*, and *The Second Coming*, Linda Hobson's interview is an appropriate place to start as it brings us back to the questions with which this essay began—*i.e.*, what sort of activity is it to devise a theory? And what are the ontological and epistemological implications of doing so? As we have seen, there are two profoundly different answers to the first of these questions. In this interview Percy plainly indicates what he would take to be the correct one:

> But are we saying that we're going to leave it to the novelists, that nobody but novelists or maybe theologians can write about these things? Or is there a way of thinking about it rationally? Getting some ordered discipline? I would like to think that sure enough you can make a model or develop a theory (which has already been done—it's been started by people like Charles Peirce) of what it is to be the organism which uses language.[2]

This remark, together with those quoted above, betrays that prejudice which governs each of the linguistic essays and is quite explicitly owned in "Toward a Triadic Theory of Meaning"—*i.e.*, the prejudice which favors a "scientific" or "rational" approach to the question of who and what a man is over a "novelistic" approach to this issue. Given the conceptual framework which upholds this conventional hierarchy, the irony of Percy's insistence upon a new model or theory with which to think about man is great indeed. He is, of course, quite right to stress the need for a new model, but what counts for him as "new" and "radical"—in this case a "semiotics of the self"—is neither. The truly radical alternative, the "novelistic" one, is suspect because it is not "rational" and lacks "ordered discipline."

The notion of a "radical science of man" exerts a powerful influence upon Percy's imagination. This we already know. But the full

1. Linda Whitney Hobson, "The Study of Consciousness: An Interview with Walker Percy," *Georgia Review*, XXXV (Spring, 1981), 56–60.
2. *Ibid.*, 57.

range of that influence becomes apparent only in "A Theory of Language" and in the otherwise innocuous Hobson interview. While the latter discloses that power with devastating economy, in the former Percy's lust for a theory of man and his lust for a radical science come together for exhaustive (and, I fear, exhausting) exposition. The result is certainly Percy's most ambitious essay. With some help from Charles Peirce's theory of abduction, he undertakes to devise "a crude explanatory model"[3] of language and, by implication, of man which will go between the horns of the dilemma posed by Chomsky *et al.* on the one hand, and Skinner *et al.* on the other. The result of Percy's strenuous efforts to achieve this goal is an essay the linguistic and philosophic sophistication of which is surpassed only by the degree to which the spirit of abstraction governs its argument. In short, "Theory" is not only Percy's most ambitious essay; it is also the one in which the suasions of the Cartesian framework are most potent and in which his complex confusion is deepest and most plainly visible.

On the other hand, we have *Lancelot* and *The Second Coming.* These two provide the perfect counterpoint to "Theory" and bear witness to the equal power of the storyteller-as-theorist. In *Lancelot* the singular form of craziness which afflicts Lancelot Andrewes Lamar and issues in mayhem on a grand scale has its roots in those very forms of abstraction which afflict Percy himself in "Theory." The important difference and the important point is that in the novel *Percy knows better.* He knows better because the instrument with which he is thinking about the world provides a perspective on that world as unavailable to the author of "A Theory of Language" as it is to the character Lancelot. *The Second Coming* reintroduces our old friend Will Barrett now middle-aged, rich, and suffering not from amnesia but from "*wahnsinnige Sehnsucht*" or "inappropriate longings."[4] His story follows logically upon the enigmatic "Yes" with which *Lancelot* ends when the priest-psychiatrist answers Lance's question, "Is there

---

3. This phrase is from the essay's subtitle, which is in full: "A Martian View of Linguistic Theory, Plus the Discovery That an Explanatory Theory Does Not Presently Exist, Plus the Offering of a Crude Explanatory Model on the Theory That Something Is Better Than Nothing." Walker Percy, *The Message in the Bottle*, 298. Subsequent references appear in the text, with the abbreviation MB.

4. This interesting diagnosis is made by one Dr. Ellis of The Duke Medical Center. Walker Percy, *The Second Coming* (New York, 1980), 302.

anything you wish to tell me before I leave?" As an answer to both Lancelot and essayist Percy, *The Second Coming* provides the perfect context in which to bring this inquiry into the joys and sorrows of symbol-mongering to a close.

In a word, "Theory" on the one hand and *Lancelot* and *The Second Coming* on the other display the most extreme schizophrenia of the imagination we have yet encountered, and so underscore the potency and ubiquity in our culture of a certain second-order account of what it is to know, to think, to be a person, a self. The "Enlightened earnestness" and extreme abstraction of "Theory" set side by side with the acuity, wit, and concreteness of *Lancelot* and *The Second Coming* confirms the thesis that Percy's strengths and weaknesses as a critic of modern Western culture and its dominant philosophic tradition rooted in Descartes are logically of a piece with the inconsistencies and contradictions of that tradition; and that it is the novel, not the philosophic essay, which provides the conceptual tools most efficacious both for disclosing the incoherence of that tradition and for developing a radical alternative to it.[5]

THE SUBTITLE OF "A Theory of Language" clearly sets forth Percy's agenda: "A Martian View of Linguistic Theory, Plus the Discovery That an Explanatory Theory Does Not Presently Exist, Plus the Offering of a Crude Explanatory Model on the Theory That Something Is Better Than Nothing." This subtitle indicates the end to which Percy aspires, why he aspires to get there, and the means by which he aims to do it. It thus provides a convenient path through the thickets of this piece beginning with the reference to a familiar figure, the Martian. The phrase "A Martian View" must immediately put us in mind of "The Delta Factor" and the problematic use to which our friendly visitor is put in that essay. There, the notion of "taking a Martian view" leads Percy astray in his reflections about man and language. Specifically, it leads him astray insofar as it constrains him to remain within the Cartesian framework, the notion of detachment synonymous with the position of the godlike philosopher in relation to the objects of his

5. The phrase "enlightened earnestness" is from William H. Poteat's essay "Reflections on Walker Percy's Theory of Language," in Panthea Reid Broughton (ed.), *Stratagems for Being: The Art of Walker Percy* (Baton Rouge, 1979), 211.

knowledge. From the first paragraph of "Theory" it is clear not only that Percy again identifies himself with the Martian but that he still holds his, the Martian's, detachment to be his chief virtue—this time in relation to evaluating the present state of linguistic theory. Professing his own "distance from and innocence of standard linguistic disciplines," he adds:

> What virtues [this essay] may have are mainly those of perspective. I do not presume to compare myself to the boy who noticed that the king was naked nor linguists to the king's subjects. Yet innocence—and distance—may have its uses. Just as a view of the earth from space may reveal patterns in forested areas and deserts which might be missed by the most expert foresters and geographers— because they are too close—so it is that what follows is what might be seen from a Martian perspective, that is to say, a perspective worlds removed from the several admirable disciplines of linguistics. (MB, 298)[6]

With this Percy discloses his "posture" in relation to the immediate topic at hand, the sorry state of linguistic theory, and by implication, to the fundamental question of the nature of man. It is both regrettable and unsurprising that he does not consider certain less felicitous implications of the Martian's sky-high vantage, implications W. H. Auden expresses succinctly in his essay "*Hic et Ille*":

> From the height of 10,000 feet, the earth appears to the human eye as it appears to the eye of the camera; that is to say, all history is reduced to nature. This has the salutary effect of making historical evils, like national divisions and political hatreds, seem absurd. . . . Unfortunately, I cannot have this revelation without simultaneously having the illusion that there are no historical values either. From the same height I cannot distinguish between an outcrop of rock and a Gothic cathedral, or between a happy family playing

6. Percy is either too modest or not entirely ingenuous here. As we shall see, he is hardly "ignorant" of "standard linguistic disciplines." Indeed, it may be his very acquaintance with these disciplines which binds him so firmly to the concepts which inform them.

in a backyard and a flock of sheep, so that I am unable to feel any difference between dropping a bomb upon one or the other.[7]

Auden's remark is very much to the point here. The perspective of the Martian which Percy so eagerly claims for himself transforms the world and its lively inhabitants into a montage of objects indistinguishable from one another. In the specific case of "Theory" and what Percy hopes to accomplish in it, the epistemological fallout from this transformation may be characterized by using Percy's own distinction between knowledge and news. I have already alluded to the difficulties in "The Delta Factor" which accrue to "taking a Martian view." The categories knowledge and news provide another way to think about these and analogous difficulties which prevail in "Theory," especially those which issue from the high premium Percy places upon the Martian's detachment. As you will recall, the *conditio sine qua non* for the acquisition of knowledge *sub specie aeternitatis* is that the knower abstract himself from his own predicament and assume the posture of objectivity in relation to what is known. He must, in a word, become Anyone, Anyplace and construe the world accordingly. Now, in claiming for himself the detached perspective of the Martian, Percy assumes a posture appropriate to the verification and extension of knowledge but not to the hearing of news. This distinction is most important, because while linguistic theory as such falls under the category of knowledge *sub specie aeternitatis* with all that that entails, the question of who and what a man is does not. In accordance with the central thesis of *The Message in the Bottle*—i.e., the place to begin in devising a theory of man is language—it is the latter Percy hopes to get at with his theory of language. The cogent argument in "The Message in the Bottle" forgotten, however, he scuttles his present undertaking by assuming the very stance (that of detached Martian) and focusing upon an object of knowledge *sub specie aeternitatis* (linguistic theory) which will together prevent his hearing any news of persons in predicaments.

The significance of "taking a Martian view" and the subsequent

7. W. H. Auden, "*Hic et Ille*," in *The Dyer's Hand and Other Essays* (New York, 1968), 101.

transformation of news into knowledge cannot be overemphasized. Logically of a piece with fixing one's eye not upon persons in predicaments but upon an explanatory theory of man, a move consistent with the Cartesian picture of the self, this strategy constitutes a choice of framework and language game. As such it pretends Percy's reflections in such a way as to limit his options for thinking about language in terms other than very abstract ones. This becomes plain as his argument progresses and we come to the second issue implicated in the essay's subtitle—*i.e.*, the charge that an explanatory theory of language does not presently exist. On the face of it this seems an odd claim. What counts for Percy as an "explanatory theory" such that neither the "structural-descriptive-generative analysis of language as a corpus" (Chomsky, Bloomfield, Harris, Fodor and Katz) nor a "plenary model of language as phenomenon" (Skinner, Malinowski, Mead, Hockett) will do? Before attempting to answer this question, it will be useful to recall Percy's critique of the behaviorist and idealist approaches to language. First, he faults these schools only insofar as they commit a sin of omission, suggesting that their respective shortcomings lie in what they leave out, not in where they started from. Second, this oversight betrays the fundamentally nonradical nature of Percy's own approach to language via the "delta phenomenon." His present critique of linguistic theory displays the same blind spot, and the "crude explanatory model" he outlines in the concluding section of the essay is equally nonradical.

The complaint Martian-Percy lodges against current linguistic theory is much the same as that put forward in "The Delta Factor": "What the Martian sees in the case of earth linguistics is a, to him at least, remarkable bifurcation of theoretical effort of such a nature that the central phenomenon is straddled—as if Speke were on one side of Lake Victoria and Burton on the other" (MB, 299). As in "The Delta Factor" Percy argues that what is missing from both transformationalist and behaviorist linguistic theory is nothing less than "the central phenomenon," man himself—man as speaker, man as actor, man as embodied self. So far so good. There is nothing controversial or problematic about this claim. The problem arises only when we consider the particulars of Percy's complaint—*i.e.*, the reasons why in his view the Skinnerians and the Chomskians do in fact miss the point; or in

Percy's idiom, the reasons why theirs is not "an explanatory theory."[8] Briefly, the particulars are these: Percy could be quite content with the learning theory of the behaviorists as an explanatory theory (it "meets all the specifications") were it not for one thing—it is wrong. How so? "S-R theory, however modified . . . fails to address itself to, let alone explain, those very features of language behavior which set it apart from other forms of animal communication"—*e.g.*, naming or "symbolization" or language acquisition by a child. What is problematic here is not Percy's criticism of the behaviorists, which is certainly well placed. Rather it is the claim that, though wrong, S-R theory is a bona fide "explanatory theory." Why, we must ask ourselves, is that? The answer lies, interestingly enough, not in what Percy says about behaviorism directly, but in his criticism of transformational generative grammar. The failure of the latter as an explanatory theory is "not a consequence of its stated objective, which is in fact correct; namely, to specify the character of the device which mediates the processing . . . of the language." Nor does it fail because of the "putative and unconfirmed status of so-called 'deep structures,' from which surface structures are derived by transformation" (MB, 304). The key phrase here is "to specify the character of the device." Presumably this is the telos of a true explanatory theory, and presumably the behaviorists with their "hard-headed empiricism" and fixation upon which synapses snap and in what order when an organism is "stimulated" and "responds" are at least on the right tract.[9]

The transformationalists must be on the right track too insofar as their "stated objective" is correct. The point at which, in Percy's view, they do fail is most significant:

8. Percy actually distinguishes between three approaches to linguistics: descriptive or structural linguistics (Harris), behavioristic learning theory (Skinner), and transformational generative grammar (Chomsky). The first he treats only very briefly, dismissing it as merely descriptive.

9. We should note if only in passing the abstract language Percy favors here describing our ordinary speech in terms of the "input" and "output" of "data." This must put us in mind of such loaded phrases as "a naming delight," "a dynamic succession of energy states," "everyday language exchanges," and Percy's persistent use of "symbolic behavior" in lieu of "speech," "language," or "conversation." We may also look forward to more of the same in "A Theory of Language"—*e.g.*, "What else indeed is the child up to for months at a time when it goes around naming everything in sight—or asking its name—than establishing these functional intercortical connections?" (MB, 326). What else? Try, "naming things."

Transformational grammar is not an explanatory theory of language as phenomenon but rather a formal description, an algorithm, of the competence of a person who speaks a language. There is no evidence that this algorithm bears a necessary relation to what is happening inside the head of a person who speaks or understands a sentence. There is evidence in fact that it does not. (MB, 304)

This is not the first time Percy has appealed to the distinction between what happens "inside the head" and what happens somewhere else ("outside the head"?) in order to establish the locus and bent of his own interest. Here this appeal sheds additional light upon the "character" of that "device," the specification of which Percy deems necessary to an explanatory theory of language—it must be "inside the head." Again, with a backward glance at Percy's comments on behaviorism, we may infer another of its putative virtues, namely, S-R theory allows us "inside the head," right there where the synapses snap and a host of S's and R's fly about the cerebral cortex. Later we learn that what Percy means by a device "inside the head" is in fact a "neurophysiological correlate" of the "semological-phonological combinations" of the two-year-old child learning to speak. This "correlate," he suggests at the very end of the essay, may be "'the human inferior parietal lobule, which includes the angular and supramarginal gyri, to a rough approximation areas 39 and 40 of Brodmann.'" (MB, 326).[10]

For the moment we may set aside the obvious question as to how this tack is different from that of the behaviorist *simpliciter* who seeks just the right neural pathway which will exhaustively "explain" human "behavior." Instead, suffice it to observe that Percy's quest for a device "inside the head," coupled with his commendation of behaviorist S-R theory (albeit "wrong"), betrays how unreflective he is vis-à-vis the repertoire of concepts which informs both the neo-Cartesian mentalism of the transformationalists and its inverse, the "modified" S-R/learning-theory reductionism of the behaviorists. In short, despite the fact that Percy knows neither model can do the conceptual work he wishes to do, he persists in using the conceptual tools those models provide, as is made plain in the substantive role played by the very

10. "Neuro-physiological correlate" appears several times in the essay. Percy draws on the work of neuroanatomist Norman Geschwind to make this final point.

problematic inside-the-head/outside-the-head distinction in both his critiques of behaviorism and transformational grammar and in the alternative model he proposes.

There is more. Percy faults transformational grammar as an explanatory theory on yet another point. It fails, he argues, because "it violates a cardinal rule of scientific explanation, namely, that a theory cannot use as a component of its hypothesis the very phenomenon to be explained" (MB, 304). Consider carefully what Percy is saying here. First, his appeal to the rules of "*scientific* explanation" suggests that a proper explanatory theory is a "scientific" one. Given the weight of "scientific" in other essays such as "Culture: The Antinomy of the Scientific Method" and in the Hobson interview, we must be wary of its appearance here. To put the matter quite simply, why must an explanatory theory of language be "scientific" and what would distinguish such a scientific theory from an "unscientific" one? The essays studied in Chapter III can help us here if we recall that in them "science"/"scientific" is virtually synonymous with "empiricism" and "empirical" and that, even though Percy regards his own empiricism as "broad and untrammeled" and "free of the dogmatic limits of positivism," he is in truth held captive by the presumption that all our feats of knowing may be exhaustively explained in terms of the empirical method. Presumably, then, a "scientific explanation" of language would be in some important sense empirical. As such, it would adhere to certain rules and procedures logically homogeneous with the empirical method of the natural sciences.

The analogy Percy uses to illustrate his point bears out this presumption:

> That is to say, if one sets out to explain the appearance of an apple on an apple tree, it will not do to suppose that apple B, which we have in hand, derives from putative apple A, which we hypothesize as its progenitor. An adequate account of the origins of either apples or sentences must contain in the one case only nonapple elements, e.g., pollen, ovary, ovule, etc., and in the other case nonsentential elements. (MB, 304)

The logical equivocation evident in this analogy is profound. Notice that Percy casts his illustration not in terms of actors and speakers but in terms of a second-order account of an "empirically ascertainable" botanical phenomenon in which an apple is transformed into an assemblage of "nonapple elements." Moreover, the ontological and epistemological monism implicit in his "equation" of apples and sentences is consistent with that evident in his delta factor triangle and in the tetradic model of "symbolic behavior" prominent in other essays. No doubt apples and sentences look alike to the Martian winging it high above the earth. To ordinary, earthbound folk, however, they seem to be rather different sorts of things and, as such, require different forms of "explanation."

Finally and most remarkable is this: What Percy is in fact suggesting—if we take him with complete and uncritical seriousness—is that *ideally* we should devise a theory of language without using language! Lest I be accused of grossly misreading Percy here, think again about what he says: "A theory cannot use as a component of its hypothesis the very phenomenon to be explained." To be sure, if asked, Percy would deny that this is what he "really" means; that language cannot be a "component" in a "hypothesis" about language. No doubt he would be speaking the truth. Rather than undermining the point, however, this response would uphold it. So thoroughly abstracted is Percy from the roots of his own speech—roots in a world in which apples (not "nonapple elements") grow on trees and are not to be confused with sentences uttered by sentient, motile men and women—he cannot see that what he has proposed is a feat of abstraction which is, on its face, logically impossible. A botanist may indeed talk about the generation of apples in terms of pollen, ovaries, and the like and perhaps, if he is not of the Laplacean persuasion, reintegrate these sundry parts in his imagination into something recognizable as an apple. But how are we to eliminate language from our reflections about language? To do so would be to accomplish the supreme feat of abstraction—better than emptying the mind of all but the most clear and distinct ideas, better than dropping out of the old modern age. To do so would be to rid ourselves of that which is most radically and irreducibly reflexive and which places us at the midpoint between angels and beasts—the power to speak, to hear, and to understand.

Such a proposal is nonsensical, but the point remains. Percy's gravitation toward an account of language abstracted from concrete situations of speaking-hearing, meaning-understanding, intending-comprehending is very clear in his appraisal of behaviorism and transformational grammar. As he goes on to outline his own "crude explanatory model," language itself does not disappear, but his argument does become increasingly abstracted from actors and speakers and increasingly intent upon the finer points of linguistic theory. That pretension implicit in the passages above becomes quite explicit in the final section of the esssay in which Percy is thoroughly engrossed in the project of "explaining" language, that which sets man apart from the merely organismic, in terms of a model which is itself fundamentally organismic.

In a very straightforward sense, Percy's explanatory model hinges upon Charles Peirce's theory of abduction, which he takes to be "nothing more nor less than the method of hypothesis formation as it is used in practice by scientists in general, whether one is theorizing about why volcanoes erupt or why people speak and animals don't." Percy goes on to say, following Peirce, that one must begin with facts and seek an explanatory theory to fit the facts, and the more simple and economical the model or theory the better. He praises this theory of abduction as "both sufficiently rigorous that it achieves the level of explanatory adequacy and sufficiently nonspecific that it does not require a commitment to ideology and hence does not fall into the deterministic trap of behaviorism and learning theory" (MB, 322).[11]

In a less obvious sense, however, Peirce and his theory of abduction are of only tangential importance here. What is of real significance is what Percy abstracts from Peirce and the end toward which he uses it. Briefly, Percy's so-called crude explanatory model looks like this: His wariness of Chomsky's mentalism notwithstanding, Percy declares his basic assumption vis-à-vis language to be that every person is "uniquely equipped with what can be characterized abstractly as a Language Acquisition Device (LAD) whose structure and function are unknown but which receives as input primary data . . . and has as its output a competence in the language." The problem, therefore, is how to approach "the black box, LAD, toward the end of discovering its workings" (MB, 320–21). He goes on to suggest that "the basic and genetically prime component of the LAD is a semological-phonological

---

11. Note the unmistakable echo of that divorce between theory and practice implicit in the claims Percy makes elsewhere for "his" empiricism.

device through which semological elements are coupled with pho-nological elements" (MB, 324). Following Peirce again, he adds that this operation is a triadic as opposed to a dyadic (*i.e.*, S-R) one. In the paradigmatic instance of a father pointing to an object and uttering the sound *balloon*, whereupon his young son looks and nods, Percy says, "An event of the order shown below must occur somewhere in-side both father and son" (MB, 324–25):[12]

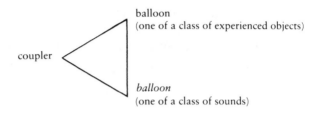

balloon
(one of a class of experienced objects)

coupler

balloon
(one of a class of sounds)

Before going on to the refined version of this triangle with which Percy concludes, it is important to note first that his entire argument is radically abstracted from any concrete situation involving speakers and hearers. We have "couplers," a "semological-phonological de-vice," "a class of experienced objects," and "a class of sounds," but no "speakers," "sentences," "things," or "words." Second, his argument still hinges upon an appeal to the highly equivocal inside-the-head/ outside-the-head distinction. Apart from the specific instances in which Percy refers to what ostensibly goes on "inside the head," the notion of an LAD rests upon the assumption that language is *funda-mentally* an inside-the-head phenomenon and could therefore be "ex-plained" if only we could figure out what goes on in the "head box." Third, the above triangle is identical in its ontological flatness to its delta factor counterpart. In place of Helen *cum* "element," we find child *cum* "coupler." The latter stands in precisely the same static, atemporal relation to balloon (one of a class of experienced objects) and *balloon* (one of a class of sounds) as does Helen in relation to *water* (word) and water (liquid). This is especially significant given

12. Compare the following, which comes at the end of his review of Peirce: "I be-lieve, however, that by the serious use of abduction, hypotheses, not the attributing of it [the grammar of a language] to the child, but the figuring out of what goes on inside the head of a child, the theorist can hope to make a start toward the construction of a rela-tively simple and parsimonious model along Peircean lines" (MB, 324).

Percy's firm belief that Peirce's triadic, as distinct from a dyadic, model of language is in itself proof against the sorrows of both Chomskian mentalism and Skinnerian S-R theory.

Perhaps the most striking thing about Percy's model is that in trying to go between Chomsky and Skinner he does not repudiate their respective approaches in any fundamental sense but rather draws heavily upon the conceptual tools essential to each—*e.g.*, Chomsky's "black box" and Skinner's "network of associative connections." The thinness of this strategy is nowhere more plain than when immediately following the above diagram, he continues:

> Let us say nothing about the physiological or ontological status of the "coupler." Suffice it for the present to say that if two elements of a sentence are coupled, we may speak of a coupler. Indeed, the behavioral equivalent of Descartes's *cogito ergo sum* may be: If the two elements of a sentence are coupled, there must be a coupler. The latter dictum would seem to be more useful to the behavioral scientist, including transformational linguists, than Descartes's because Descartes's thinking is not observable but his speech is. (MB, 325)

What are we to make of such a statement? First, if Percy's model avails us nothing in terms of understanding "the physiological or ontological status of the 'coupler,'" then what does it avail us? Perhaps being "useful to the behavioral scientist" is, in Percy's view, sufficient. If so, then not only has he fallen short of his professed goal but he is simply mistaken. As William Poteat observes, "it is only by specifying this [the ontological status of the coupler] that our conceptual orientation can be established to the diagram in which it appears. . . . Without this guidance we are, where the diagram is concerned, left with very close to the complete abstraction: black triangular figure on a white ground."[13] In effect, Percy's "Let us say nothing . . ." is an invitation to become the paradigmatic Anyone, Anyplace. As we know,

13. Poteat, "Reflections on Walker Percy's Theory of Language," 213. Poteat adds another important point: "And if reference is made to the words about the pointing father and the nodding boy as the exegetical device for interpreting the diagram, then we are once again openly faced with the question as to how the former is overlaid on the latter, which is to raise precisely the question about the ontological status of the coupler." *Ibid.*, 213.

such a one is in no position to hear news from across the sea. Second, we must be wary of any "equivalent" to the Cartesian *cogito ergo sum*. The dubious desirability of an "equivalent" picture of the self is rendered even more problematic when the precise meaning of the word is not at all clear. The final sentence of the paragraph, no doubt intended to enlighten us on this very point, can only increase our uneasiness. When Percy suggests that the virtue of his equivalent lies in the fact that speech is "observable" while thinking is not and that it (his "equivalent") is therefore more "useful," we must realize that we are once again in the company of that problematic concept of the "real" ("as real as . . .") discussed at length in Chapters I and III.

In an interview focusing specifically on "Theory," Percy rephrases this last statement in a way that reveals just how profoundly confused is his theory of language. He claims that the main flaw in Descartes' conception of the *Cogito* is "you can't see Descartes thinking and so you can't prove his self." [14] "To prove the self" is the real telos of Percy's "crude explanatory model" and indeed of all his linguistic essays. The equation here between "to see" and "to prove" is logically homogeneous with his fixation upon the "observable" and the "empirically ascertainable," which notions carry much weight in the linguistic pieces. This homogeneity betrays the extent to which Percy's model relies heavily upon the epistemological values of behaviorism. It also betrays the extent to which the telos of his model is not news but knowledge *sub specie aeternitatis*. As such it is subject to the verification procedures consonant with that category of communication.

What is most important about Percy's wish "to prove the self" is that the need for "proof" arises at all. Only an imagination held captive by the dictum "reject as being absolutely false everything in which [you] could suppose the slightest reason for doubt" [15] could make such a proposal and then attempt to carry it through. The great irony of this agenda should be plain: Implicated in the very effort to locate a neurophysiological correlate of man's unique ability to speak *and*

14. Marcus Smith, "Talking About Talking: An Interview with Walker Percy," *New Orleans Review*, V (1976), 13. In this same interview, Percy makes another telling remark when he says he kept "A Theory of Language" as "empirical and linguistic" as possible in order to avoid "metaphysics." *Ibid.*, 14.

15. René Descartes, *Discourse on Method and The Meditations*, trans. F. E. Sutcliffe (Baltimore, 1968), Discourse #4, p. 53.

thereby "prove" the self is that either/or choice Percy is at such pains to dismantle in his fiction—*i.e.*, the self is either *essentially* an angel or *essentially* a beast. In short, Percy's explanatory model bears the unmistakable imprint of one afflicted as is that scientist who, near the end of *Love in the Ruins*, has the misfortune to receive a dose of heavy sodium ions to the "pineal body, seat of self": "Forever after he'll live like a ghost inhabiting himself. He'll orbit the earth forever, reading dials and recording data and spinning theories by day, and at night seek to reenter the world of creatures by taking the form of beasts and performing unnatural practices" (LR, 370). Having launched himself into the upper regions inhabited by couplers, semological-phonological devices, classes of experienced objects, etc., the "unnatural practice" is, in this case, seeking to reenter the ordinary world and recover "that ordinary self, the restless, aching, everyday self, the secret self one happens on in dreams, in poetry, during ordeals, on happy trips," by entering into the "human inferior parietal lobule, which includes the angular and supramarginal gyri to a rough approximation areas 39 and 40 of Brodmann" (LR, 370; MB, 326). The prognosis is not good.

Thus by the time we arrive at the "refined" triangle I mentioned earlier, we are on very shaky ground indeed. Drawing on the work of Norman Geschwind, Percy suggests that the human inferior parietal lobule may be the neurophysiological correlate he seeks. It meets the two principal specifications—*i.e.*, it is of relatively recent evolution in the human brain and "structurally and functionally triadic in character with the base of the triad comprising what must surely be massive interconnections between the auditory and visual cortexes." If Geschwind's findings are correct, Percy adds, then "what he has uncovered is the cortical 'base' of the triadic structure of the typical semological-phonological naming sentence." This structure is diagramed as follows:

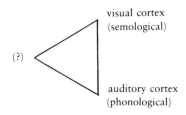

He then concludes: "The apex of the triangle, the coupler, is a complete mystery. What it is, an "I," a "self," or some neurophysiological correlate thereof, I could not begin to say" (MB, 327).

What then, the reader might well ask, has Percy said? The question mark at the left of the final diagram, together with Percy's concluding sentence, seems to indicate that we have little to show for his—and our—strenuous efforts to wrest a coherent theory of man from the incoherence of current linguistic theory. Percy's attempt to suture Chomsky's black box onto the human inferior parietal lobule tells us only that together these two are even more conspicuously unhelpful vis-à-vis Binx's still unanswered question than they are singly. What Percy has succeeded in doing is all too unsurprising, given the ubiquity in our culture of a certain second-order account of knowing governed by the spirit of abstraction. He has repeated in his own imagination the ruinous cast made, paradigmatically, by Descartes and embodied in the very language of what is held to be our culture's highest achievement, modern science. In so doing, "he found the Archimedean point, but he used it against himself; it seems he was permitted to find it only under this condition." [16]

It must be quite clear by now that when Percy sets out to devise a theory of language in this essay, the model of theory he has in mind is the regnant one. As a result and despite efforts to the contrary, he, no less than Chomsky in his way and Skinner in his, finally misses the issue central to any *coherent* theory of man and language, namely, what is the ontological status of the speaker?; or, what does it mean to be a castaway and wait for news from across the sea? We must conclude that he misses the point not because he lacks a certain expertise in linguistic theory—*i.e.*, not because he lacks this or that bit of island knowledge—but because in the context of the highly abstract philosophical essay, he has not the conceptual tools appropriate to it. What nevertheless redeems Percy's effort from the ranks of the trivially confused and places it in the select company of the profoundly confused is the degree to which his failure stems from an acute awareness of the

---

16. Franz Kafka, quoted by Hannah Arendt in *The Human Condition* (Chicago, 1958), 248. Arendt does not cite the original source but does give the original German: "*Er hat den archimedischen Punkt gefunden, hat ihn aber gegen sich ausgenutzt, offenbar hat er ihn nur unter dieser Bedingung finden dürfen.*"

limits of what we may loosely term "the scientific method" *together with* a deep-rooted bondage to the second-order account of reality abstracted from that method. Most obvious in Percy's determined pursuit of "a radical science of man," that bondage is embodied in the very words and images he chooses to present his argument. This last point is most important. It is crucial to realize that "to present an argument" is not an exercise abstracted from reality but one which shapes reality. Moreover, words, images, rhetorical strategies—all the linguistic elements of a given language game—bear a reflexive relation to the one who uses them. Thus is the self shaped even as it shapes its world. So it is with Percy in "A Theory of Language"; so it is with Percy in his fiction. In the former, however, he adopts the sky-high vantage of the Martian and the only conceptual tools at hand are ones which can survive in that rarified atmosphere. Those which can are ones which render Martian-Percy unable to distinguish between a flock of sheep and a happy family, between an outcropping of rock and a gothic cathedral, between "establishing functional intercortical connections" and "naming things." They likewise make news over into knowledge and ensure that the castaway will not heed the newsbearer's "Come!" should it be spoken.

IN THE SAME article in which he makes his throw-away remark about the opening of "The Delta Factor," Hugh Kenner waxes equally cryptic about the last sentence of "A Theory of Language" quoted above: "That's a sentence about you and me. There's a novel in it."[17] Indeed there is—two novels to be exact, as I shall show in the remainder of this chapter. Between the violent madness of Lancelot and the gentle strangeness of Will and Allie, Percy's two most recent novels depict the extremities of action and affection available to us denizens of the postmodern age. What gives these novels their singular incisiveness and polemical power is not only Percy's characteristic feel for the telling detail and his equally characteristic wit. Like the first three novels, *Lancelot* and *The Second Coming* display an acute awareness of the toll so relentlessly exacted from the human spirit by all that makes the modern age peculiarly "modern"; or more precisely, by the basic

17. Hugh Kenner, "On Man the Sad Talker," *National Review*, XXVII (September 12, 1975), 1002.

incoherence of our dominant philosophic tradition, which offers little possibility for understanding the embodied self. What sets *Lancelot* and *The Second Coming* apart in this respect is the nearly unrelieved darkness and violence of the former set over against the hard-won peace of the latter. It is as though Percy has come to a new and urgent awareness of both our peril and our hope. To these two, then, we shall turn and at last bring our reflections to a close.

Lancelot Andrewes Lamar might be described as a perverse analogue to the scientist in *Love in the Ruins* who is utterly abstracted from himself and seeks to reenter the ordinary world by engaging in "unnatural practices." In this case, the unnatural practice is murder. Lance seems genial enough at first: "Come into my cell. Make yourself at home. Take the chair; I'll sit on the cot." Ever the obliging host, he begins his long monologue with this invitation to his old friend, priest-psychiatrist Percival, who has come not to speak but to listen. Appearances can be deceiving, of course, and from the first there is a strong undertow in Lance's story, an undertow which becomes stronger and more deadly as his madness rises to the surface and the violent act which put him in a "Center for Aberrant Behavior" is disclosed.[18]

The discovery which prompts Lance to murder four people, including his wife, is the discovery that she was unfaithful to him years before and that his ten-year-old daughter is not his at all. His act, terrible as it is by any standard, would not be *peculiarly* so if he acted out of extreme but rather ordinary rage. His reaction, however, is another thing altogether. He compares it to that of an astronomer who finds a dot out of place on one of his photographic plates: "*Hold on. Hm. Whoa. What's this? Something is wrong. Let's have a look*" (L, 19). What Lance feels is not an "appropriate" emotion—e.g., shock, humiliation, anger—but interest. Speaking always to the silent Percival, he continues:

> Yes, interest! The worm of interest. Are you surprised? No? Yes? . . . The only emotion people feel nowadays is interest or the

18. Walker Percy, *Lancelot* (New York, 1977), 3. "Center for Aberrant Behavior" is nicely ambiguous and we never learn if it is more prison than hospital or vice versa. Similarly, we do not know until the very end that Percival is really a priest; we never know for certain if he is also an M.D. Nor can we be sure that the intent of Lance's father was to name him after the sixteenth-century divine, Lancelot Andrewes, or if he really had in mind Lancelot du Lac, King Ban of Benwick's son. The implicit confusion of piety, adultery, and violent death is quite appropriate.

lack of it. Curiosity and interest and boredom have replaced the so-called emotions we used to read about in novels or see registered on actor's faces. Even the horrors of the age translate into interest. . . . When was the last time you saw anybody horrified? (L, 21–22)[19]

Lance is quite perceptive here. His own "interest" in Margot's adultery, like that of the person who reads the headline PLANE CRASH KILLS THREE HUNDRED with interest rather than horror, is not only grossly inappropriate but a more common phenomenon than we might like to think. What is really significant about his reaction, however, is that only a man utterly abstracted from himself could feel nothing more than this when confronted with what should properly be a very personal trauma. There is in fact nothing at all personal about his reaction; "the worm of interest" is a nameless, neutered creature which may be taken up and put aside at will.

Later Lance makes the following observation about the movie makers who are Margot's guests and soon to be his other victims. (One of them, Merlin, is allegedly the father of daughter Siobhan.)

The actors, I noticed, took a light passing interest in everything, current events, scientology, politics. They were hardly here at all, in Louisiana that is, but blown about this way and that, like puffballs, in and out of their roles, "into" Christian Science, back out again. (L, 112)

What Lance fails to realize is how closely he resembles these people who are certainly the most unappealing characters in all of Percy's fiction. Like the actors in their way and the astronomer in his, Lance too stands over against the world and its inhabitants as one who has abstracted himself out of his predicament and is ontologically "blown about." Thus for him, what should properly be the *news* of a grave offense against his person is transformed into a piece of knowledge *sub specie aeternitatis.* Consequently, Lance's actions from that point forward are the actions of a man whose posture in the world is identical with that of the scientist intent upon solving an abstract problem

19. It is worth remembering here that near the end of "A Theory of Language," Percy introduces the hypothesis of neuroanatomist Gerschwind "as a matter of interest only" (MB, 326).

and giving no thought to his own predicament. "I had to know," he says. "If Merlin 'knew' my wife, I had to know his knowing her. Why? I don't know. . . . I only knew for the first time in years exactly what to do. I sent for Elgin" (L, 90).[20]

Lance becomes obsessed with knowing. Even knowing the worst, even defeat, is preferable to not knowing. Moreover, his way of knowing is abstracted from action ("One has to know for sure before doing anything. . . . I have to be absolutely certain.") and has the effect of reducing all and sundry to electrons, molecules, data. Logically of a piece with Lance's "interest" and his self-proclaimed kinship to the astronomer, this reductionism becomes more marked as his madness increases in intensity and destructive power. Early on he describes Margot's intercourse with Merlin as "taking a small part of Merlin's body into her body. . . . Nothing more is involved than the touch of one membrane against another. Cells touching cells" (L, 16–17). When he discovers that his daughter Siobhan's blood type "did not compute," he reduces the "problem" to a series of "equations," "calculations," "arithmetic" involving "four pieces of data." The worm of interest turns.

It is still turning later when Elgin, an electronics wizard for whom there is no greater joy than problem solving, gives him the video film of overnight traffic in Margot's and the actress Raine's rooms. When he delivers the film, made in secret, of course, the young man is apologetic about the quality of the images:

> "It's a negative effect I can't explain."
> "Negative effect?"
> "Did you ever hold a magnet against a TV screen?"
> "No."
> "It pulls the images out of shape—the images being nothing but electrons, of course."
> "Yes, electrons."
> "I only watched enough to see that the effect is a little weird—

20. Robert D. Daniel alludes to Percy's distinction between knowledge and news and goes on to make a similar observation: "Lancelot's insistence on knowing where one stands reduces human choices to a scientific problem." See Robert D. Daniel, "Walker Percy's *Lancelot*: Secular Raving and Religious Silence," *Southern Review*, XIV (Winter, 1978), 191.

But I think you may have what you want."
"Thank you." (L, 181)

I quote this exchange in full because the "negative effect" Elgin describes does indeed give Lance what he wants, a dehumanized scenario
in which everything is turned inside out—light becomes dark, life becomes death, Lance becomes God. The figures, he observes, are very
badly distorted and "seem to be blown in an electronic wind. Bodies
bent, pieces blew off. . . . I stared. Didn't Elgin say the figures were
nothing but electrons?" (L, 185–86). Lance's description of the scene
in Raine's room reduces the figures even further: "Pieces of bodies,
ribs, thighs, torsos, fly off one body and join another body. . . .
Mouths and eyes open on light. Light pubic triangles turn like
mobiles, now narrowing, now widening, changing from equilateral triangles to isosceles triangles to lines of light" (L, 191).

Strictly speaking, the distortion in the film is not Lance's doing. It
is, however, quite congenial to his imagination. This is implicit in the
passages referred to above and becomes quite clear when, picking up
on the stark physics and geometry of what he sees, Lance begins drawing diagrams—first, two triangles depicting the *ménage à trois* of
Margot, Merlin, and himself, then Margot, Merlin, and Jacoby, her
new lover; second, stick figures representing the threesome in Raine's
bed: Raine, actor Dana, and his older daughter Lucy. Given Percy's
own fondness for diagrams, the temptation to seize upon these as
proof that Lancelot "is" Percy is great indeed, and, in one *limited*
sense, to do so would be correct. The abstraction which issues in
Lancelot's diagrams is logically of a piece with that which issues in
Percy's own in *The Message in the Bottle*. As Lancelot reduces a complex human situation to black lines on white paper, so does Percy re-
duce Helen Keller's great discovery to three "elements" depicted in a
one-dimensional triangle. The real importance of this analogy, however, lies in the point at which it breaks down. As the creator of the
insane Lancelot, Percy is well aware of the dangers of the abstraction
and reductionism represented in these static, atemporal figures. This is
clear not only from the bad, sad end to which Lance comes, feeling
cold and dead and empty—not to mention the fates of Margot *et al.*—
but most important, in the silent listening presence and eventual

speech of Percival. I shall return to this point later, but for the present we should remember that Lance's is not the only voice in this novel.

His lust for knowledge satisfied and, as Auden would put it, all historical values wiped out and the human reduced to the merely material, only murder remains. Having sent everyone but Margot, Raine, Dana, and Jacoby away (everyone including Merlin, interestingly enough), Lance very methodically sets out to blow Bell Isle into oblivion. So far gone is he that even this act is carried out in a most detached way. Finding Margot and Jacoby together in bed, he sees them as a "beast," a "succubus," and when he cuts Jacoby's throat, he feels absolutely nothing:

> What I remember better than the cutting was the sense I had of casting about for an appropriate feeling to match the deed. . . . I remember casting about for the feeling and not finding one. . . . Not even the knife at his throat seemed to make any difference. All it came down to was steel molecules entering skin molecules, artery molecules, blood cells. (L, 242, 254)

This violent act carried out in this abstracted way is logically consistent with reducing the complexly human to the merely anatomical or geometric or molecular. For Lance it is, as Robert Daniel puts it, "an easy step from sex as molecules rubbing to murder as molecules separating."[21] Thus does the worm of interest turn upon others and, by so doing, turns in the end upon itself.

There is another theme woven into Lance's monologue which further elucidates the nature of his madness. Just as Chomsky is the inverse of Skinner, so is a preoccupation with the infinite the inverse of reductionism. In the case of Lance, this preoccupation manifests itself at the juncture of what he calls his quest for the "unholy grail," a true sin, and his plans for the future, for a "Third Revolution." Now, before we hear anything about either a quest or a Third Revolution, Lance turns to the subject of woman—not *a* woman but "She. Her. Woman. Not a category, not a sex, not one of two sexes, a human female creature, but an infinity. $♀ = ∞$" (L, 129). From this perspective, "Love is infinite happiness. Losing it is infinite unhappiness." "What

21. *Ibid.*

else," Lance asks, "is man made for but this?" In this loose talk about "infinity" and "absolutes" in connection with woman, love, and sex, Lance is transacting some serious conceptual business. At no point is he able to think concretely, to think in terms of an ordinary, mortal woman and ordinary, finite, Wednesday–morning love and sex. Instead, he has a demonic obsession with the boundless and the absolute, with boundless good and absolute evil. Seconds before her death Margot says to him, "That's what you never knew. With you I had to be either-or—but never a—uh—woman" (L, 245). With this simple declaration, the ill-fated woman puts her finger on that turn of mind and disposition of heart which at once makes it possible for Lance to murder coolly four people and impossible for him to look into his own heart and see that "Evil is unspectacular and always human, / And shares our bed and eats at our own table, / And we are introduced to Goodness every day, / Even in a drawing-room among a crowd of faults."[22] To place both good and evil squarely between the infinitely great and the infinitely small—which is to say, squarely in the heart of a man—is a feat of which the mad Lancelot is incapable.

It is this terrible obsession which determines both the nature of Lance's quest and his plans to build a new society. As to the former, he says:

> Sin is incommensurate, right? There is only one kind of behavior which is incommensurate with anything whatever, in both its infinite good and its infinite evil. That is sexual behavior. The orgasm is the only earthly infinity. Therefore it is either an infinite good or an infinite evil.
>
> My quest was for a true sin—was there such a thing? Sexual sin was the unholy grail I sought. (L, 139–40)

This quest which lumps sex, sin, woman, infinity, good, and evil brooks no interference from ordinary folk who do not fit into Lance's either/or categories. So too with the predicted Third Revolution. In his new society, men will be stern, pitiless Galahads perfect in honor and bravery. As for women, the New Woman will have "perfect freedom. She will be free to be a lady or a whore" and a man "will know who to

22. W. H. Auden, "Herman Melville," in *Collected Shorter Poems, 1927–1957* (New York, 1967), 145–46.

fuck and who to honor" (L, 179). On and on Lance goes. He who would ascend to the lofty reaches of the "infinite" condemns himself as one who knows neither love nor forgiveness but for whom the secret of life is violence and rape and its gospel is pornography; for whom man is "a thinking reed and a walking genital" (L, 223); and who, when Percival apparently remonstrates with him, replies, "You are pale as a ghost. What did you whisper? Love? That I am full of hatred, anger? Don't talk to me of love until we shovel out the shit" (L, 179). If we must depend upon this man to save us, then we are in more trouble than we knew.

Thus does Lancelot reach for the extremities of the infinitely great and the infinitely small, absolute good and absolute evil, angel and beast. For him there is no middle place where an ordinary man may be born and live and die, suffering ordinary griefs and rejoicing in ordinary blessings. There is no place in his world for the ambiguities of the merely human. All is either buggery or niceness, wonderful or evil, and a woman is either a virgin or a whore. Thus to sunder self and world is logically homogeneous with Descartes' division of the self into thinking thing and extended thing and his reduction of the world to the status of mere object. It is this division and this reduction which gives us, paradigmatically, the either/or choices Lance himself would give us—either/or and nothing else.

What then of the silent Percival? Near the end of "The Message in the Bottle" Percy says, "Sometimes silence itself is a 'Come!'" So it is with Percival, whose silence grows "louder" as Lance waxes more grandiose and more violent in his monologue. Though the listener does not actually speak until the very end, Lance often alludes to his friend and auditor in such a way as to record Percival's reactions to what he is saying. He, Percival, is alternately amused, pensive, preoccupied, sorrowful, and increasingly horrified—yes, horrified, not interested. This last takes hold when Lance begins to talk about his plans for a Third Revolution, his hatred and anger almost palpable. By the time Percival speaks, Lance has begun at last to reap the bitter fruit of his lust for knowledge and for the infinite:

> But there is one thing . . . There is a coldness . . . You know the
> feeling of numbness and coldness, no, not a feeling, but a lack of

feeling. . . . I don't feel anything—except a slight curiosity about walking down that street out there. . . . I feel so cold, Percival. (L, 253)

Even so, he remains opaque to himself and to his own responsibility for what has happened. Only Percival's voice can jolt him out of his fascination with his own hatreds.

Just before Percival speaks, however, Lance has one more deed to do. He commits that "true sin" which he sought in others with such disastrous results. It is not a sexual offense but a repetition of the Original Sin, the sin of pride:

> If God does not exist, then it will be I not God who will not tolerate it. I, one person. I will start a new world single-handedly or with those like me who will not tolerate it. But the difference between me and God is that I won't tolerate the Russians or the Chinese either. God uses instruments. I am my own instrument. (L, 255–56)

And what does Percival plan to do while Lance is re-creating the world in his own image?: "So you plan to take a little church in Alabama, Father, preach the gospel, turn bread into flesh, forgive the sins of Buick dealers, administer communion to suburban housewives?" (L, 256). While Lance has been either musing about steel molecules cutting into skin molecules or meditating on the proposition " $\female = \infty$," Percival has quietly arranged to go forth into the old, fallen, worn-out but familiar human world to seek the lost and minister to them. Like Binx Bolling who aims to hand people along and be handed along in turn, like Tom More who gives up his lust for the Nobel and learns to watch and to wait and to listen, like Father Boomer in *The Last Gentleman* who administers last rites to Jamie Vaught, like Will and Allie in *The Second Coming* who shun the tempting comforts of illness and insanity and reach out for the ordinary warmth of one another— like each of these, Percival will go forth to Alabama and do whatever work is needed there. At this point, he looks straight at Lance and answers his questions clearly and without hesitation, "Yes" or "No." Thus we are told that while the world is indeed in a sorry state, Lance's way of changing it is not the only way. He will make a new beginning with Anna, the woman in the room next door, but that beginning may not be in the form of a Third Revolution after all. Lance then asks one final question and with it the novel ends: "Very well. I've finished. Is there anything you wish to tell me before I leave?" "*Yes.*"

The importance of Percival's speech here at the end lies not only in what he says, which is significant in terms of suggesting an alternative to Lance's own "future plans." It lies equally in the fact that Lance's monologue becomes, if only briefly, a dialogue. Percival's silent presence is of course important throughout as just that—a silent presence, an other who might at any time speak and thereby appear. When he does speak, however, a significant change occurs in the whole economy of Lance's world. The nature of that change can best be understood by recalling a passage from Arendt's *The Human Condition* quoted in Chapter I. I think it worth repeating here:

> To men, the reality of the world is guaranteed by the presence of others, by its appearing to all; "for what appears to all, this we call Being," and whatever lacks this appearance comes and passes away like a dream, intimately and exclusively our own but without reality.[23]

When Percival speaks, the reality that is guaranteed by others is made available to Lance as it has not been before. Hearing only the sound of his own voice, Lance's life is like a dream, intimately and exclusively and violently his own but having no purchase in any world shared by others except that they are his victims. Percival's speech changes all that, creating a space of appearance apart from which the apprehension of truth, of reality itself is impossible. Only thus is Lance brought back to earth able at last to listen because he is confronted by "an Otherness that can say *I*."[24] Only thus may he learn that the world is not either buggery or niceness, wonderful or evil, but something complexly, ambiguously, intractably in between. Only thus can he learn that by virtue of being a denizen of such a world he is a person in a grave predicament whose salvation lies not in making a new world

23. Arendt, *The Human Condition*, 199. It is worth noting that, thanks to some pills given him by Raine and the narcotic effect of the methane which fills the house, Lance is literally in a dreamlike state when his obsessions flower at last into murder.

24. W. H. Auden, *For the Time Being: A Christian Oratorio*, in *Collected Longer Poems* (New York, 1969), 176.

single-handedly, but in the much harder task of learning to watch and to wait and to listen in the old.

Lancelot is unquestionably Percy's darkest work. It also displays a remarkably clear fix on the complex relation between the conceptual underpinnings of modern culture and the actions of individual men. Once again, we find Percy in firm command of issues which elsewhere bring him to grief. Lance's lust for knowledge as distinct from news, his reductionism, his obsession with the infinite are all demons we have seen loosed upon essayist-Percy with equally serious if less dramatic consequences. Embodied in Lancelot, however, they can be seen for what they are and, like the ravening particles, be got around. Thus Percy does indeed *know better* as the creator of Lancelot Andrewes Lamar than as the creator of an abstract theory of language *cum* radical science *cum* semiotics of the self. Once again, as instruments for reflection about what it is to be a man and to live and die, the tools of the storyteller prove superior to those of the philosophical essayist. These same tools are used with equal felicity to tell the happier tale of Will Barrett and Allison Vaught Huger in *The Second Coming*. No "high tale of love and death" theirs but rather a quiet tale of love and life hard-won and finite and good.[25]

QUITE APART from the fact of Will Barrett's reappearance in *The Second Coming*, it is worth recalling one of the two epigraphs to *The Last Gentleman*, a passage from Romano Guardini's *The End of the Modern World*. I quote it in full:

> We know now that the modern world is coming to an end. . . . At the same time, the unbeliever will emerge from the fogs of secularism. He will cease to reap benefit from the values and forces developed by the Revelation he denies. . . . Loneliness in faith will be terrible. Love will disappear from the face of the public world, but the more precious will be that love which flows from one lonely person to another. . . . the world to come will be filled with animosity and danger but it will be a world open and clean.

25. This is from the first line of Joseph Bedier's *The Romance of Tristan and Iseult*: "My lords, if you would hear a high tale of love and death . . . ." Trans. Hillare Belloc and Paul Rosenfeld (New York, 1965), 3. The allusion is, I think, quite appropriate to Lance's story.

This passage makes an excellent bridge from *Lancelot* to *The Second Coming* in that the first part would serve very well as an epigraph for the former and the second ("Loneliness in faith . . .") as an epigraph for Will's and Allie's story. More than anything else theirs is indeed a story of the love that flows from one lonely person to another, and it is upon them and the life they make together that we shall focus.

When the novel opens we discover that Will Barrett did not marry Kitty Vaught and go into the Chevrolet business after all. Instead, he took himself north to law school and Wall Street, married a plain, cheerful, and *very* rich Yankee girl, took early retirement, and settled down to live on his wife's estate near the mountain resort town of Linwood, North Carolina, where he does good works and plays golf. When the story begins, Will's wife has recently died and he has taken to falling down on the golf course, remembering with perfect clarity persons and places forgotten for thirty years, and worrying about the supposed emigration of all North Carolina Jews to Israel. Even worse, he has developed a terrible slice in his golf swing. Vance Battle, physician and golf partner, is worried.

Allie meanwhile has just escaped from a private mental hospital of dubious distinction. She is the daughter of Kitty and, like Kate Cutrer in *The Moviegoer*, has been proclaimed "unstable" and "sick." She is in fact a perceptive and resourceful person albeit somewhat halting of speech and spotty of memory thanks to repeated electric shock treatments. Allie has made her way to Linwood to claim her inheritance, eight hundred acres of land adjacent to the golf course where Will is routinely slicing out of bounds. The house on the place has long since burned and she makes her home in the only remaining structure, a fine turn-of-the-century greenhouse, all glass and copper, which backs up to the steep side of the mountain. She does not realize it at first but this last is no mere quirk. The greenhouse was built against a vent in a large system of caves so as to catch the air, a steady 60°F year round. This fact becomes most important later, but for the present, with a large and easily embarrassed dog for company and a great Grand Crown stove for warmth, she sets out to make a new beginning.

On the face of it, these two make a most unlikely pair and between them have more than a few problems. Whereas Lancelot is crazy and obsessed with sex and death, Will is crazy and obsessed with God and death. His introduction to the latter came early when his death-dealing, death-loving father tried to kill himself and his son. He later succeeded with respect to himself and the now middle-aged Will is haunted by these memories. He is not his father's son for nothing, and the temptation to be as he was and do as he did is strong:

> Did you not believe, old mole, that these two things alone are real, loving and dying, and since one is so much like the other and there is so little of the one, in the end there remained only the other?
>
> Silence.
>
> Very well, old mole, you win. (SC, 162)

Will has many such "conversations" with "old mole" and seems drawn inexorably toward the same end his father suffered. This penchant for death both informs and complicates his other obsession, namely, a quest for God. After some reflection, Will makes "the Great Discovery": "It dawned on him that his father's suicide was *wasted*. It availed nothing, proved nothing. . . . It was no more than an exit, a getting up and a going out, a closing of a door" (SC, 182). Will is determined not to make the same mistake and concocts an outlandish scheme by which he will enter the caves under the great mountain and, like a latter-day Job, demand that God break his silence. He describes this "scientific experiment" in a long letter to Sutter Vaught:

> I shall go to a desert place and wait for God to give a sign. If no sign is forthcoming, I shall die. But people will know why I died: because there is no sign. The cause of my death will be either his nonexistence or his refusal to manifest himself, which comes to the same thing as far as we are concerned. . . . Will it not be a relief to all of mankind to have this dreary question settled once and for all, proved or disproved? (SC, 193)

"So it was that Will Barrett went mad."

Fortunately, Will's wait for God or starvation, whichever came first, is abruptly brought to an end by, of all things, a terrible, nauseating toothache. As the narrator dryly observes, "There is one sure cure for cosmic explorations, grandiose ideas about God, man, death, suicide, and such—and that is nausea. I defy a man afflicted with nausea to give a single thought to these vast subjects. A nauseated man is a sober man. A nauseated man is a disinterested man. What does a nauseated person care about the Last Days?" (SC, 213). As a stricken Barrett puts it, "Let me out of here." We cannot help but laugh at Will's sudden abandonment of his grandiose plans all because of a toothache, and that is as it should be. But his quest is in deadly earnest and we would do well to pay attention. Will looks about him and discovers that believers and unbelievers are equally crazy and unattractive. He wonders why, if the good news is true, no one seems especially pleased to hear it, not even the Christians. He wonders why his daughter, who claims to have been born again and talks a lot about love, is the angriest person he has ever known. He recalls how his wife often spoke of the joys of marriage, family, etc., etc., and wonders why such talk always made him glum. He is also full of wonder to find that "only with death and dying does the sharp quick sense of life return" (SC, 126). In short, Will Barrett's radar is as keen as ever and he finds much amiss with himself and his fellows. What he does not realize, however—and in this he is much like Tom More—is that no "scientific experiment" can resolve these contraries and complexities. The questions he asks are beyond the pale of the scientific method or any strange appropriation thereof. Too, Will would have done well to remember that when God finally breaks his silence and speaks to Job out of the whirlwind, it is not to answer but to question.

Allie's problem has nothing to do with God or death or sex or any such grand thing, but with language—not theories of, mind you, but with the ordinary business of speaking: "Words surely have meanings, she thought, and there is my trouble. Something happens to my words. They do not seem worth uttering" (SC, 82). Most problematic, however, is the silence that falls in between the words, "a silence in which something horrid takes root and grows. What if nobody says anything, what then? Sometimes she thought she had gone crazy rather than have to talk to people. Which was worse, their talk or their silences?" (SC, 108). This is not a minor difficulty and Allie feels her way with care. Her speech is indeed singular by conventional standards but, despite its oddness, has a clarity and richness all its own. For example, when Will brings avocados and a small can of Plagniol, she expresses her pleasure saying, "What a consideration! But more than a consideration. The communication is climbing to the exchange level and above. And the Plagna is not bologna" (SC, 109). Later when he offers to fetch men to move the stove for her she refuses: "Because there I will be with people having put the stove where I want it. And that's the old home fix-up which is being in a fix. Then what? The helping is not helping me" (SC, 112). Unlike her parents and psychiatrist, Will has no trouble understanding Allie and can interpret her "slow, scanning speech" to others. This is one of the bonds between them.

Slowly, carefully Allie makes her way. She cleans the greenhouse, cares for the dog, learns to hoist with pulleys, block and tackle, and moves and installs the stove herself. In physical labor and in careful speech, she grows in strength and confidence and lays claim to the self that had long ago been sundered from itself by the pressures of ordinary living and had been kept up, "buzzed up" as she calls it, by her treatment at the hospital. She is much better when Will crashes into the greenhouse through the vine-covered cave vent.

Though this is not their first nor even second meeting, Will's unintentional intrusion into Allie's glass house marks a turning point for both. When Will falls out of the cave and quite literally into Allie's arms, he knows what to do: "take care of people who need taking care of. . . . Then we'll see" (SC, 265). He has also learned the name of the enemy and it is death, "not the death of dying but the living death" (SC, 271). He is determined that unlike his father he will not be defeated by it: "You gave in to death, old mole, but I will not have it so. It is a matter of knowing and choosing. To know the many names of death is also to know there is life. I choose life" (SC, 273–74). To know and to choose and to act: Will's real "Great Discovery" is that these three are within his power. Even so, he still falls down from time to time and needs to be hoisted. Allie is a hoister.

For her part, Allie is stronger in body and spirit, but before Will's sudden appearance she admits that things had begun to slip a little, that "looks became impaling." The hardest is getting through the "yellow spent time" of late afternoon. Of this time she says to the dog:

This time of day is a longens.
The dog turned his anvil head first one way then the other.

What?

In this longitude longens ensues in a longing if not an unbelonging.

What? said the dog. (SC, 238)

Allie still needs an interpreter. Will is an interpreter. She needs someone to remember things and he remembers everything. Most important, however, "with him silence didn't sprout and looks didn't dart" but "one plus one equals one and oh boy almond joy" (SC, 263). Will makes Allie happy.

Thus Will Barrett and Allie Vaught Huger make several important discoveries in cave and greenhouse. Their difficulties are not over— e.g., Will's daughter hustles him off to Duke and Dr. Ellis and then installs him in a convalescent home; Allie's parents learn where she is and threaten to send Dr. Duk and the sheriff to fetch her back to the hospital—but they survive these unwanted and misguided attentions. Because of a raging toothache and the quiet love of Allie, Will avoids Lance's fate. He still seeks God but not in death, not in "cosmic explorations," not in violence, but in the love of a woman and the face of an elderly, unprepossessing priest who, nevertheless, speaks with authority. Barrett recognizes a newsbearer when he hears one:

> Will Barrett thought about Allie in her greenhouse. . . . His heart leapt with a secret joy. What is it I want from her and [Father Weatherbee], he wondered, not only want but must have? Is she a gift and therefore a sign of a giver? Could it be that the Lord is here, masquerading behind this simple silly holy face? Am I crazy to want both, her and Him? No, not want, must have. And will have. (SC, 360)

With these questions and this declaration, *The Second Coming* ends. Into this brief passage are woven all that will sustain Will Barrett in his new life, his second coming. Mark how very different these things are from the grand resolutions he took with him into the cave. Will has put aside neither his search for God nor his deep wariness of "the living death." What has changed, however, is that these two are now grounded in ordinary love, ordinary work, and an ordinary confusion of faith and waywardness. Thus does Will come again into life and love; thus does Allie find her own voice and self. Together they will make not a perfect, heroic life but one of falling down and getting up, of forgetting and remembering, of odd speech and skillful interpretation. Thus together will they await another Second Coming foretold by those of whom Father Weatherbee is the successor. They will wait knowing full well that, as the poet says, "the Time Being is, in a sense, the most trying time of all."[26]

IT IS IN his presentation of "the Time Being" that Percy's theory of man is most clearly and persuasively argued. Nowhere is this more the case than in *Lancelot* and *The Second Coming*; nowhere is it less so than in "A Theory of Language." When Percy is in the world as storyteller, the Time Being is his framework and there his theory of man must find voice and body. When he is in the world as philosopher, the Time Being does not exist and a theory of man must find habitation in some other framework—and does in the Cartesian *Cogito*. Only the first, however, can even begin to disclose who and what we are, because it is in the Time Being that we live and die, that we speak and act and know and love. While neither Percy nor any other one save a newsbearer "of divine origin" can tell us so much as is folded into the declaration "For unto us a child is born," he can and does keep faith with this news. He does so by reminding us that to be a man and to live and die is to hear the news and yet not hear it, to anticipate the Fullness of Time even as we are bound to the Time Being; by reminding us that we are neither angels nor beasts but men and as such must be reconciled in and to a fallen world, an imperfect self.

In the *Journals* Kierkegaard writes:

> Usually the philosophers (Hegel as well as the rest), like the majority of men, exist in quite different categories for everyday purposes from those in which they speculate, and console themselves with categories very different from those which they solemnly discuss. That is the origin of the mendacity and confusion which has invaded scientific thinking.[27]

---

26. Auden, *For the Time Being*, in *Collected Longer Poems*, 196. This line is from the narrator's final speech and the sentence reads in full: "To those who have seen / The Child, however dimly, however incredulously / The Time Being is, in a sense, the most trying time of all."

27. Søren Kierkegaaard, *The Journals of Søren Kierkegaard: A Selection*, ed. and trans. Alexander Dru (London, 1938), Paragraph #582, p. 156.

This state of affairs is exactly what we find when we set "A Theory of Language" side by side with *Lancelot* and *The Second Coming*. In the former Percy "solemnly discusses" language and in so doing embodies the deepest sorrow of symbol-mongering—the power of words to perpetuate rather than to heal the hurts of the riven self. In the latter he attends from and to the lived life and in so doing touches the greatest joy of symbol-mongering—the power of language to free us from the limits of "flesh poor flesh" even as it makes its home in that very flesh without which it would be naught. Thus in our words do body and spirit find equal welcome.

At the juncture of this sorrow and this joy, we find Percy even as we find ourselves. We must conclude that, in Kierkegaard's words, it is by the "categories" embodied in his fiction, woven into the very words and images and metaphors he uses, that he lives and "consoles" himself, just as in the end it is by those embodied in Allie and the old priest that Will Barrett must live—not by the ones implicit in his "scientific experiment." If it were otherwise, Percy would not have the power to write of Lance and Percival and Will and Allie as he does. He would not have the power because he would know nothing of the sorrows they suffer or the joys that redeem them; to such as these, the Martian is blind and deaf. We can only be glad that Percy is neither.

Epilogue

It is true that storytelling reveals meaning without committing the error of defining it, that it brings about consent and reconciliation with things as they really are, and that we may even trust it to contain eventually by implication that last word which we expect from the "day of judgement."

HANNAH ARENDT
Men in Dark Times

WALKER PERCY is a serious writer. By "serious" I do not mean merely "sincere" or "earnest" or even "highly skilled"—though he is surely all of these. Rather, I mean that Percy is perceptive enough and steadfast enough to ask simple questions which strike at the complex heart of our culture and our selves: Why does man feel so sad in the twentieth century?; What is it to be a man and to live and die? Moreover, he asks these questions as one firmly convinced that the conceptual antecedents of our culture—most particularly, that picture of the self expressed, paradigmatically, by Descartes—are not of an arcane and abstract nature and therefore of interest only to professional philosophers and academics. Rather, as his novels and certain of his essays make abundantly clear, he perceives quite rightly that the mind-body dualism of Descartes and all that follows from it penetrates our lives at every turn. No one escapes, certainly not Percy himself.

It is this last which makes his work worth a long and careful look. The fact that one so unfailingly on the mark as a novelist should go so far wrong as a philosophical essayist is in itself striking. But when we find that Percy's confusion in the essays is no less profound than his insight in the novels, then we are brought face to face with issues which bear directly upon those "simple" questions alluded to above, namely, our commonly held notions of what it is to think, to know, to devise a theory; what we mean by "clarity"; what we take the self to be; and not least, what we take to be the nature of truth and of reality itself. All this Percy brings to us and it is a rich repast indeed.

Not only is Percy a serious writer. He is a religious one as well. What do I mean? It is, of course, a commonplace that Western culture underwent a profound change in the seventeenth century. One of the more devastating aspects of that change was that we in the West lost our sense of place. Suddenly, the earth was no longer the center of the universe and, by implication, man was no longer the center of God's attention. He was instead, as Pascal realized with harrowing clarity, absolutely alone, confronted by the terrifying, empty spaces of a universe that knew him not.

This upheaval was a deeply religious one and not merely in the sense that God was no longer securely stationed in heaven. The English word *religion* comes from the Latin *religāre*, meaning to bind again, hence, to bind strongly. Thus we might infer that religion is that which strongly binds a man to reality; that which is the source of his deepest sense of who and what he is and, without which, his world lacks coherence and meaning. This sense of coherence and meaning was lost to us in the European Enlightenment. Artists and philosophers alike have been trying to recover it ever since.

In this sense, Walker Percy is a profoundly religious writer. Feeling in his own bones the crack-up that wrenched soul from body, he seeks, as Tom More puts it, a way to reenter the world "whole and intact man-spirit"; a way "to weld the broken self whole." His successes and his failures together reveal the nature and depth of the *religious* dilemma which is the legacy of the Enlightenment. Perhaps even more important, however, they disclose the singular power of storytelling to bring about consent and reconciliation "with things as they really are." To do this is no small thing.

Like Arendt, Percy is "onto" this singular power and, when he is in the world as storyteller, wields it with great skill and finesse. So it is that from him we may learn what it is to be a castaway and wait for news from across the sea. And if the newsbearer comes and speaks to our predicament with perfect sobriety and in good faith? "Well, then, the castaway will, by the grace of God, believe him." [1]

1. Walker Percy, *The Message in the Bottle* (New York, 1975), 149.

INDEX